MW00973283

THE
FAMILY VALUES
MOVEMENT

PROMOTING FAITH THROUGH ACTION

The Abolitionist Movement

The Civil Rights Movement

The Environmental Movement

The Ethnic and Group Identity Movements

The Family Values Movement

The Labor Movement

The Progressive Movement

The Women's Rights Movement

REFORM MOVEMENTS
IN AMERICAN
HISTORY

THE

FAMILY VALUES
MOVEMENT

PROMOTING FAITH THROUGH ACTION

Samuel Willard Crompton

Series Editor
Tim McNeese

CHELSEA HOUSE
PUBLISHERS
An imprint of Infobase Publishing

Cover: Although the American family has changed a good deal from the days of Norman Rockwell, it is still an important component of American society.

The Family Values Movement: Promoting Faith Through Action

Copyright © 2008 by Infobase Publishing

Chelsea House
An imprint of Infobase Publishing
132 West 31st Street
New York NY 10001

Library of Congress Cataloging-in-Publication Data
Crompton, Samuel Willard.
  The Family values movement : promoting faith through action / Samuel Willard Crompton.
     p. cm. — (Reform movements in american history)
  Includes bibliographical references and index.
  ISBN-13: 978-0-7910-9608-6 (hardcover)
  ISBN-10: 0-7910-9608-4 (hardcover)
  1. Family—Moral and ethical aspects—United States—Juvenile literature. 2. Social values—United States—Juvenile literature. 3. United States—Social conditions—Juvenile literature. 4. United States—Moral conditions—Juvenile literature. I. Title. II. Series.
  HQ536.C774 2007
  306.850973'0904—dc22

                                        2007026476

Series design by Kerry Casey
Cover design by Ben Peterson

Printed in the United States of America

Bang EJB 10 9 8 7 6 5 4 3 2 1

This book is printed on acid-free paper.

All links and Web addresses were checked and verified to be correct at the time of publication. Because of the dynamic nature of the Web, some addresses and links may have changed since publication and may no longer be valid.

CONTENTS

1

The America of Norman Rockwell and Robert Bly

Everything changed between 1940 and 2000. Nothing changed between 1940 and 2000. Each of these statements is at least half right. Change, or the lack of change, depends on perspective, which is largely influenced by one's generation: the time, place, and situation into which one is born and reared. Let's examine what American family life was like in the 1940s, a time preserved for us by an artist's paintbrush.

THE HOMECOMING

Born in 1894, Norman Rockwell was 51 when he painted *The Homecoming*, which became the cover of *The Saturday Evening Post* in late May 1945. In the painting, clothes hang on a line, and neighborhood children frolic in a tree. Mother stands on the stoop, her arms open wide. Father looks up from his carpentry, a grin spreading across his handsome, though weather-beaten, face. Brother leaps from the porch, his long legs working like pistons. Sisters gape, openmouthed, at their returning hero. Grandfather stands in the background, puffing on his pipe.

Our eyes stray to the girl next door. She stands shyly in the shade provided by a nearby building, but we notice her white dress and guess that she will soon play a large role in the life of the returning soldier. He stands with his back to us, his army clothes slightly rumpled. Although we cannot see his face, we suspect it shows an immense longing mixed with satisfaction. The soldier has done his best in World War II and is now thrilled to be home. It is May 1945. Millions of American boys, recently turned into men by the fires of war, are about to come home.

Image and Reality

Born and raised in New York City, Norman Rockwell did not grow up in the type of rural village setting he liked to depict. He was enamored of this existence, nonetheless, and painted hundreds, if not thousands, of scenes from American life, beginning around 1916. Rockwell did his best to paint the virtues and values, as well as the comic absurdities, of life in rural America. How he succeeded!

At least two generations of Americans enjoyed Rockwell's portrayal of everyday life: mostly those who were adults in the period between about 1920 and 1970. *The Saturday Evening Post* was one of the most successful periodicals of the time, and everyone discussed Rockwell's homespun painting style. Critics disparaged Rockwell's artistic talent and said that he was making a fortune turning out second-rate copies of work that would only have earned a "B" rating in the past. Admirers said that Rockwell understood America and its people, especially its families, better than any other artist of his time.

There was one point that both critics and admirers missed. Rockwell was painting an America that had indeed existed, but American society was gradually changing during his lifetime. At the time of his birth, in 1894, Americans had been a predominantly rural people. The U.S. Census of 1920,

During his lifetime, American artist Norman Rockwell produced more than 4,000 original works, many of which graced the cover of the weekly magazine *The Saturday Evening Post*. Rockwell was especially known for his idealistic portrayal of the American family, including this 1943 illustration titled *Freedom from Want*, which was inspired by a speech President Franklin D. Roosevelt gave defining his four principles for universal rights.

however, showed that more than 50 percent of Americans lived in cities or suburbs, and that percentage was only to increase in the decades that followed. Was Norman Rockwell's view of the family accurate?

In 1945, the year Rockwell painted *The Homecoming*, he was still in step with the times, but just barely. Americans continued to think of themselves as a rural people, and they admired the values of wholesome country living, even as they became more urban in character each year. Rockwell's vision of America was accurate for the first third of his life (he died in 1978), was beginning to change during the second third, and was decidedly outdated in the last three decades. Perhaps it is not coincidence that *The Saturday Evening Post* went out of favor in the 1960s and ceased circulation entirely in 1971. This great periodical had served its purpose, but its time had come and gone. Let's now fast-forward (a very modern expression) from 1945 to 1996.

ROBERT BLY'S AMERICA

Born in Minnesota in 1926, of Norwegian descent, Robert Bly grew up in an area that celebrated its rural existence, similar to the towns that Rockwell painted. He served in World War II, and he could have easily been the returning soldier in *The Homecoming*. Well known as a poet and a translator of poetry, especially of the German poet Ranier Maria Rilke, Bly turned his hand to prose in the 1990s, publishing *The Sibling Society* in 1996.

Bly was no unvarnished critic of the 1930s and 1940s. He grew up in those decades and knew there was plenty of hypocrisy and unfairness prior to the great changes brought about by the 1960s and 1970s. Bly did see one great value, however, that had existed in his youth and that seemed especially absent in 1996 America: the prominence and importance of elders.

In the America that Norman Rockwell knew, and the one in which Robert Bly had grown up, elders were important in any number of ways. Before television, Americans tended to spend more time with each other, especially in the family living room. In those days, young people read or played games, and grandparents, aunts, and uncles often told them stories, poems, and jokes. Reverence is probably too strong a word, but respect was widespread. In a day and age when vaccinations were not yet commonplace and many people died young, it was no small feat to enter one's seventh or eighth decade of life. Older people were valued, in part because they were more rare than they are today.

Then, too, there was less competition. There were no televisions, computers, or cell phones, and most people lived in small circles where they were able to form close attachments with other people. Without the distractions of modern appliances and conveniences, it was more natural for young people to bond with elders in pre-1940s America. This, of course, does not mean there was little or no conflict. Many a great American novel was written about the need to leave home and escape the close quarters imposed by the American family of that time. When he looked back at his youth from the vantage point of the year 1996, however, Robert Bly saw much that had been lost. He called his book *The Sibling Society* to describe the great social change that had taken place between his youth and his old age. First and foremost, he lamented the loss of The Father and used capital letters to emphasize the importance of this concept:

> We are not talking of the wisdom of father-power but merely of the extent of it. If we look at a family in, say, Salem, Massachusetts, in 1750, the father was the Navigator in social waters; he was the Moral Teacher and Spiritual Comforter; he was the Earner, who brought in the income and kept the family alive; he was the Hearer

Pictured here in 1991, author Robert Bly believes that today's Americans are part of a sibling society in which children and adults are on an equal plane. Bly bemoans the fact that the father (and mother) no longer carry out traditional parental roles, such as moral teacher and comforter.

of Distress as well; cares were brought to the mother and then to him. People imagined the family as a Hebraic unit, as if the children were all children of God, and the house a tiny house of Abraham.[1]

So what happened?

According to Robert Bly, the American family suffered the loss of The Father sometime in the nineteenth century. As rural life became less financially rewarding, and as jobs opened up in factories and offices, men began to leave the home for at least eight hours a day to make money in those places:

> For a time during the mid-nineteenth century, then, mothers became the sole center of the family. Many devotional meetings took place in the family, the heat

of devotion entered the house, and the mothers taught inclusiveness, compassion, and self-restraint. We can feel the reality of such households in Mark Twain's novels. Mother was the Navigator in social waters, the Moral Teacher and Spiritual Comforter, and the Hearer of Distress. In most families the husband remained the Earner.[2]

Mother remained the center of the home for about 100 years, but during the middle and late twentieth century, she too left the home to become an earner. As a result, young people at the end of the twentieth century, said Bly, were left without comforters, navigators, and hearers of distress.

What happens in a society where the adults are not present? According to Bly, that society falls into a state where everyone views each other on an equal plane, as siblings, and no one has the power of an elder, a teacher, or guide. Bly claimed that one of the salient features of the Sibling Society was the desire to appear young. No one valued the gray hairs and wrinkled brows of age:

> In many ways, we are now living in a culture run by half-adults. . . . We are always under commercial pressure to slide backwards, toward adolescence, toward childhood. . . . "People look younger all the time." Photographs of men and women a hundred years ago—immigrants for example—show a certain set of the mouth and jaws that says, "We're adults. There's nothing we can do about it." By contrast, the face of Marilyn Monroe, of Kevin Costner, or of the ordinary person we see on the street says, "I'm a child. There's nothing I can do about it."[3]

One does not have to agree with Bly's entire argument to see that he is at least half correct. Adults of all ages in the United States today try to look younger than they are, and young people do not return the favor, by trying to look older than they are.

OUR AMERICA

Imagine that it is the 2010s, and a soldier has just come home from a far-off conflict. Unlike the Norman Rockwell scene in *The Homecoming*:

No clothes hang on the line, because they are in the indoor clothes drier. Few neighborhood children swing from trees; they are busy inside with their computers. Mother is indeed overwhelmed with joy to see her son, but she has a business meeting in two hours, one that she absolutely must attend. Father is not home, but he has left a video greeting, which can be displayed on the family entertainment set. Brother and sisters are delighted to see their conquering hero, but they find him a little outdated.

The pretty girl next door has not waited for the soldier's return. She has left the neighborhood, if one can call it that these days, and is pursuing a career in the big city.

There is no Norman Rockwell today. Plenty of artists have his talent, but American culture has changed so much that the life of the American family is no longer appealing to depict.

Technically, Americans are still the same. Boys still pursue girls, teenagers still grow to be adults, and most families have to work for a living. On the other hand, Americans are today a semi-urban people with a nostalgic view of their rural past, yet thoroughly disconnected from their rural past.

What happened to the American family and the American neighborhood? Where might it go from here?

2

Baby Boomers and Their Parents

Imagine reading a book on infant and child care that declared:

There is a sensible way of treating children. Treat them as though they were young adults. Dress them, bathe them with care and circumspection. Let your behavior always be objective and kindly firm. Never hug and kiss them, never let them sit in your lap. If you must, kiss them once on the forehead when they say good night. Shake hands with them in the morning. Give them a pat on the head if they have made an extraordinarily good job of a difficult task. Try it out. In a week's time you will find how easy it is to be perfectly objective with your child and at the same time kindly. You will be utterly ashamed of the mawkish, sentimental way you have been handling it.[4]

This quote is from *Psychological Care of Infant and Child*, written by John B. Watson, Ph.D. The book was published by W.W. Norton in 1928, and was one of the standard manuals for child rearing during the two decades that followed. Given that the hero in the Norman Rockwell painting in Chapter 1 was in his early 20s, it is quite possible his parents had read Dr. Watson's book, because hundreds of thousands did.

THE BABY BOOM

Today we are so accustomed to hearing about the baby boom and baby boomers that it seems as if the phrase must have described one of the defining moments of American society. The term first appeared in *Life* in 1941, as a patriotic description of how American mothers were having more children than German ones. *Baby boom* now refers to a very distinct part of American history: the generation of children born between 1946 and 1964.

Let the numbers tell part of the story:

Year	Number of Live Births in the United States
1945	2,858,000
1946	3,411,000
1947	3,817,000
1948	3,637,000
1949	3,649,000
1950	3,632,000
1951	3,820,000
1952	3,909,000
1953	3,959,000
1954	4,071,000
1955	4,097,000
1956	4,210,000
1957	4,300,000
1958	4,246,000
1959	4,244,796
1960	4,257,850
1961	4,268,326
1962	4,167,362
1963	4,098,020
1964	4,027,490[5]

We now know that the baby boom declined after 1964, but there was no way for the parents and policy makers of that time to know that until a few years had passed. In the

After the end of World War II in 1945, the U.S. economy experienced unprecedented growth that allowed many families to have more children. Known as the baby boom, this demographic upswing lasted from 1946 to 1964 and resulted in the birth of approximately 79 million children. The increased postwar birthrate caused many classrooms to be overcrowded, one of which is depicted in this photograph from the 1950s.

meantime, they had to act as if the American population would continue to grow at this fantastic rate.

PARENTS AND DR. SPOCK

In 1945 and 1946, millions of young American men came home from World War II. They were exhausted from intense conflict and hoped, in all sincerity, that their efforts had helped create a better world. Generations seldom act as uniform blocks, but the World War II veterans (henceforth referred to as the G.I. Generation) almost did so; many got married shortly after they returned and had as many children as they could support.

It is hard to say what young American women thought of the great change brought about by the return of the G.I.s. Many American women had worked in farms, factories, and offices during World War II, and most of these women lost their jobs when the veterans came home in 1945 and 1946. Some American women may have felt some resentment, but most Americans felt joy that World War II was over and that life could return to normal.

From the chart on page 16, one can see that the baby boom meant that there was a great increase in the number of live births recorded after 1945. Between 1945 and 1946, for example, the number of live births jumped from 2,858,000 to 3,411,000, an increase of 19.3 percent. Although some of the years show a slight decrease from the previous year, 1959 was the first year that precise statistics were available. Numbers never tell the whole story, but we are confident from anecdotal reports, as well as from the statistics, that this increase was sparked by the return of war-weary soldiers, who benefited from a booming economy. But how were they to raise these new babies, the 3.4 million of 1946, the 3.8 million of 1947, and so on? Dr. Benjamin Spock answered that question.

Born in New Haven, Connecticut, in 1903, Benjamin Spock was the son of a prosperous attorney, whom he revered as a powerful and distant figure, and a homemaker mother. His mother had many strong opinions about child rearing; among other things, she was an ardent believer in exposing her children to fresh air. Spock was fortunate to be too young to serve in World War I and too old for World War II. In between the two wars, he worked a bit on the Canadian Railroad, was a member of the 1924 U.S. Olympic rowing team, and earned a bachelor's degree from Yale and a medical degree from Columbia.

Dr. Spock was a powerful presence, standing six foot four, and blessed with plenty of energy. Spock became a pediatrician in New York City in the 1930s, and when approached by Pocket Books, he agreed to write a book on the care of babies and toddlers. The result was *The Common Sense Book of Baby and Child Care.* Published in paperback by Pocket Books and in hardcover by Duell, Sloane, and Pearce, this book made its mark immediately, selling three-quarters of a million copies in its first year alone. Spock's opening words indicated that his book would not be in the tradition of Dr. John Watson's:

> You know more than you think you do. Soon you're going to have a baby. Maybe you have him already. You're happy and excited, but, if you haven't had much experience, you wonder whether you are going to know how to do a good job. . . . Don't take too seriously all that the neighbors say. Don't be overawed by what the experts say. Don't be afraid to trust your own common sense. Bringing up your child won't be a complicated job if you take it easy, trust your own instincts, and follow the directions that your doctor gives you. We know for a fact that the natural loving care that kindly parents give to their children is a hundred times more valuable than their knowing how to pin on a diaper just right, or making a formula expertly.[6]

By contrast, in 1928 Dr. Watson had written: "No one today knows enough to raise a child."[7]

Dr. Spock was clearly more in line with the accepted wisdom of 1946, but he also helped create that philosophy, most especially through his relaxed, common-sense guide to baby and child care. His book was packed with information about all sorts of necessities and duties, but he wrote with an engaging sense of humor and managed to cover the subject rather thoroughly in 527 hardcover pages (By contrast, Dr. Watson's book was only 196 pages.) Spock clearly argued for a child-centered manner of childrearing. He favored breast-feeding over bottle-feeding and encouraged parents to show as much love as they could to their young children. This approach directly conflicted with the ideas of Dr. Watson.

It is clear that Dr. Spock won the battle of the books: *Baby and Child Care* went on to sell more than 20 million copies during the next 30 years, and it has never been out of print.

1940s AND 1950s VALUES

Writers like Benjamin Spock did not mention family values because it was, at the time, assumed that most Americans shared a similar moral and ethical code. A rather remarkable book was published in the same year as *Baby and Child Care*, however, that did address family values. Although *Understanding Marriage and the Family* was an academic book, written by a consortium of experts and probably read mostly by experts, it had profound things to say about the changes then underway in American life:

> As women have increasingly taken jobs outside the home, they have had more experience similar to those of men. They compete with men in business; they increasingly, but still far from equally, control property. . . . Through her power to earn and to live independently, woman has been able to throw off the more military features of male authority in the home, to secure a divorce when dissatisfied with marriage, and to avoid marriage altogether without serious impairment of status.[8]

The authors of *Understanding Marriage and the Family* did not realize that the next decade and a half, from 1945 to 1960, would be a time of retrenchment for American women. During this time, they would stay at home more often than during the World War II years, and they would often become more, rather than less, dependent on the men in their lives. The authors were accurate, however, when they spoke of a connection between family values and democracy:

> Because the crust of civilization has broken through in so many places [here they referred to World War II] we need to think realistically about the foundations of life for

individuals, for families, and for the world. . . . The home is a place where the roots of life are nourished, and upon the spiritual vitality of homes the well-being of the nation and the world depends. Peace and good will are dynamic things, based ultimately upon our total pattern of life and the kind of people we are. There must be greater attention to the quality of life in all homes and to the safeguarding of the spiritual values if even the material ones are to be preserved. [9]

Few people in 1946 disagreed with this kind of statement, but they were not overly concerned with the state of the American family. They were more worried about America's safety in an increasingly dangerous world full of threats from Communist powers. Although the Soviet Union had been a close ally to the United States during World War II, the cold war began between 1946 and 1947, and the two countries had different political viewpoints. Consequently, the two countries became engaged in a heated confrontation to win support from other countries. Americans grew increasingly concerned about China, which would indeed fall into Communist hands in 1949. The authors of *Marriage and the Family* understood these fears, and some of their writing made a direct link between family values and the strength and vitality of democracy:

Parents are trying increasingly to achieve a democratic relationship not only with each other but also with their children. Democracy at home, with its deeper understandings and its more complete participation of every member of the group, enriches the family and also serves as an indispensable preparation for democratic experience in the wider world. . . . Democracy means inner loyalty to a reciprocal relationship and guidance by the total wisdom of the group.[10]

Even as Americans became more worried about possible enemies abroad, they welcomed into their homes something that seemed friendly, even harmless, which would eventually become enormously controversial.

TELEVISION

In the early twenty-first century, television has become such a basic, fundamental aspect of American life that it is difficult to believe that people ever lived without it. Although some Americans still do not have cell phones or Internet connections, very few people do not own a television set. Indeed, the type of transistor technology that made television possible led to all sorts of other technological breakthroughs, including the creation of cell phones and the Internet. Nonetheless, most Americans did not have television until 1950 and it was not until 1955 that half of American households had TV sets. Television did not become truly ubiquitous until the 1960s.

Some might say that because fewer people had television sets at first, the early television programs were less important than the ones that came later, but the opposite is true. As television has become so widespread, and as the number of cable television stations has increased, people pay less attention, proportionally, to the big programs of today than to those of the 1950s and 1960s. There was less competition in the 1950s, so the few programs that became truly popular were indeed influential, and they helped shape Americans' views of themselves, especially their family lives. For most people who watched television in the 1950s, *Leave It to Beaver* had the deepest impact.

Debuting in October 1957, *Leave It to Beaver* featured Ward and June Cleaver and their two sons, Wally and Theodore (Beaver), living in a pleasant, indeed immaculate, suburban home. Ward Cleaver has a white-collar job in a downtown Mayfield office, but the viewer gained almost no

The television sitcom *Leave It to Beaver*, which debuted on CBS on October 4, 1957, portrayed the ideal American family of the 1950s. Pictured here from left to right are the show's cast members: Tony Dow (Wally), Barbara Billingsley (June), Hugh Beaumont (Ward), and Jerry Mathers (Beaver).

insight into his work or his personality. The show focused instead on the adventures and mishaps of the two boys. Sometimes they forgot their lunch money, or they had to earn money for a Boy Scout camping trip; sometimes they did something a bit naughty, for which their father and mother scolded them. The immensely popular program never showed a truly painful moment or bad day in the lives of the Cleavers. Their suburban life seemed to sail along merrily most of the time, with just the occasional hint of difficulty. It is safe to say there was no misfortune.

Almost anyone who watched *Leave It to Beaver* in the 1950s or who has since watched the reruns, knows that this is not what life is really like. Whether in the 1950s or in the first decade of the twenty-first century, parents have to work hard to keep their domestic ship afloat. Children have fun, to be sure, but they are also being prodded toward adulthood. What matters here is not whether *Leave It to Beaver* accurately depicts the American family of the 1950s, but the fact that this was the American family that people wanted to see and the carefree life they hoped to enjoy. Image is not reality, contrary to what advertising executives tell us, but it does help to mold reality: We do tend to see what we want to see.

THE CONFORMIST DECADE

As the 1950s began to wind down, so did the baby boom. The number of live births per year had remained strong for an astonishingly long time, but by the mid-1960s the birthrate began to drop. Toward the end of the 1950s, quite a few social critics began to criticize the state of American society. Americans were far too "Leave It to Beaverish," they declared, and there was too little concern about the state of the environment, the nation, and the wider world. This was a time of conformity.

Today, in hindsight, we can say this was not the case. Great social, demographic, and even psychological changes were actually at work during the 1950s, but they did not become prevalent until that very tumultuous decade simply known ever since as the Sixties.

3

Everything Comes Apart

The 1960s

So much happened during the 1960s that it is difficult to decide when the decade truly began. Was it the election and inauguration of John F. Kennedy in late 1960 and early 1961, or was it the appearance of the Beatles on the Ed Sullivan Show in February 1964? Which was more important: the art and music of the time, or the controversy over the Vietnam War? Most people who study the Sixties have different answers to these questions, but there was one thing that truly affected family values in this decade: the arrival of the Pill.

BIRTH CONTROL

As recently as the beginning of the twentieth century, women throughout the world had very little access to birth control. Although women had devised all sorts of methods over the years to reduce the chance of pregnancy, they nearly always remained at risk if they engaged in sexual intercourse. Most young girls were warned from early adolescence about how unwanted pregnancy would change their lives. The pioneering activities of Margaret Sanger had made new types of birth control available beginning in the 1920s, but none was as successful or as popular as the oral contraceptive pill, commonly known as the Pill, first introduced in the spring of 1960.

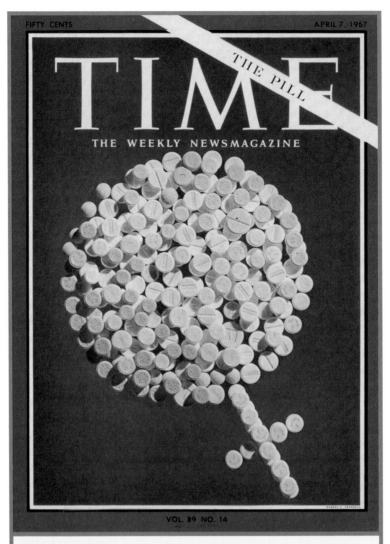

The combined oral contraceptive pill, commonly known as "the Pill," was first approved for use in the United States by the Food and Drug Administration (FDA) in 1960. By 1967, when this issue of *Time* hit newsstands, millions of women were using the Pill.

When the U.S. Food and Drug Administration approved the birth control pill that May, it did not realize how soon it would become a staple of American life. Three years later, perhaps 200,000 young American women used the Pill; by the end of the decade, millions of women used it. These women already lived rather different lives from those of their mothers, and especially their grandmothers, many of whom had worked in factories during World War II. Life in the United States was changing, and the biggest changes affected women.

THE FEMININE MYSTIQUE

Three years after the advent of the Pill, and in the same year that President John F. Kennedy was assassinated, Betty Friedan wrote *The Feminine Mystique*, which shook many women to their core. Chapter 1, entitled "The Problem That Has No Name," began:

> The problem lay buried, unspoken, for many years in the minds of American women. It was a strange stirring, a sense of dissatisfaction, a yearning that women suffered in the middle of the twentieth century in the United States. Each suburban wife struggled with it alone. As she made the beds, shopped for groceries, matched slipcover material, ate peanut butter sandwiches with her children, chauffeured Cub Scouts and Brownies, lay beside her husband at night—she was afraid to ask even of herself the silent question—"Is this all?"[11]

Friedan had not lived what anyone would call an oppressed life. A 1942 graduate of Smith College, she worked for a while before she married a successful theater producer. Some of the duties she mentioned, such as chauffeuring children and buying groceries, would not have seemed burdensome to women in the 1930s, the decade of the Great Depression. Many women identified with Friedan's words, just the same, and *The Feminine Mystique* became a best seller; it has never been out of print since the first edition was published in 1963.

Friedan explained that American women were unhappy because doctors, pediatricians, psychologists, and psychiatrists had deceived them when they said simply to "glory in their own femininity."[12] This meant that being a woman was so special that women did not need to seek fulfillment in a career, in being a homeowner, or in any number of other activities that were generally the province of men. Most of the doctors who gave this advice were themselves men, and Betty Friedan had become increasingly skeptical of their position on the matter.

Along with many of her readers, Friedan was convinced that life and work outside the home was vital for the well-being of most American women. Deprived of the social prestige afforded to American men, American women were languishing, and the one clear remedy was for them to reenter the workforce; in fact, in 1942, the year Friedan graduated from Smith College, a great number of American women were working. Friedan had hoped for a modest response to her book, but she was surprised it made her the leader of the feminist movement, which gained prominence in the 1960s, thanks in part to her book.

Feminism gained many adherents in the 1960s. Gloria Steinem, another Smith College graduate, became one of the more modern leaders of this new movement. Younger than Friedan and decidedly more feminine in appearance, Steinem argued vigorously for women's equality in all public venues. In the first few years of the feminist movement, Steinem and Friedan seemed to gain few new followers, but by the late 1960s, the feminist movement began to develop a large following. One major Supreme Court ruling after another affirmed the necessity of equal treatment for the sexes. By the early 1970s, newspapers could no longer separate classified advertisements for male and female jobs, and potential renters or homebuyers could take sellers to court for discrimination based on gender difference. At the same time, many new words entered the American lexicon: *sexist* (sometimes *sexist pig*), *male chauvinist*, and *sister*, meaning "supporter of the feminist movement." To the average American male who was not directly affected by the feminist movement, it seemed as if this woman had abruptly become empowered.

There were some critics of the feminist movement. It took some time, but by the late 1960s, Phyllis Schlafly had become one of the most important leaders of the opposition. On the surface, Schlafly's life seemed quite similar to Friedan's. They were both about the same age, college educated, and from families where women were well respected. Where Friedan railed against the oppression of women by the "feminine mystique," however, Schlafly praised that mystique, saying it was the major defense of women everywhere. What husband, she asked, would labor long and hard to provide for a family if his wife acted like a man? What children would wish to be raised in a family where both parents seemed to "wear the pants?" What would happen to American society as a whole? Might Americans go the way of the Communist Russians, who seemed determined to create a unisex society?

WAR IN SOUTHEAST ASIA

Even as feminism was hitting its stride, young Americans became equally interested in another controversial matter of the day: the war in Vietnam. As the first baby boomers turned 20 in 1966, they were old enough to be drafted for military service. Many of their peers were already halfway across the world in South Vietnam and many more would join them through compulsory military service. How the United States became embroiled in the war between North and South Vietnam is a long and tangled story, with accusations and counteraccusations coming from both

A DAY IN NOVEMBER

Millions of Americans recall September 11, 2001, the day when two planes crashed into New York City's Twin Towers and another plane hit the Pentagon, outside of Washington, D.C, as the single most searing moment of their lives. That event started the "War on Terror." Older Americans, however, also remember another important day that had a large impact on American society: November 22, 1963.

On a sunny afternoon in Dallas, Texas, President John F. Kennedy was shot and killed as his motorcade progressed through the city. Police quickly found the apparent assassin, Lee Harvey Oswald, but Jack Ruby, a Dallas nightclub owner, murdered him shortly after he was apprehended. Months of investigative work followed, capped by a congressional committee that ruled that Lee Harvey Oswald had acted alone, and that he was the sole person involved in President Kennedy's death. Whether or not this is true has been hotly debated over the decades, but the Warren Commission's verdict still stands.

What matters here is not so much who killed President Kennedy, but the circumstances of his death, and the way he has been remembered ever since. Born in 1917 and educated at Harvard University, he was not

sides. American involvement in Vietnam began during the Republican administration of President Dwight Eisenhower (1953–1961), and it continued during the Democratic administration of John F. Kennedy (1961–1963). There might have been a moment for the United States to pull back from Vietnam shortly after Kennedy's assassination in November 1963, but his successor, Lyndon B. Johnson, continued and accelerated the previous commitment to help the democratic South Vietnamese government against the communist North Vietnamese.

The first baby boomers went to war in 1965 and 1966, and 2 million of them served in Vietnam during the next a typical American by any means, but he had tremendous charisma, which made it seem as if he were indeed "one of us." Handsome, charming, and remarkably witty, President Kennedy became deeply loved during the thousand days of his presidency, and at his death there was an outpouring of sentiment by many Americans.

Kennedy's widow, Jackie, with the couple's two children, stood by the casket at the funeral. Millions of Americans watched on television as the Kennedy family appeared to be the model of heroic behavior. Kennedy's assassination and the weeks that followed made the Kennedy family into America's family, and they retained that distinction for many years to come.

One can certainly ask: Would Kennedy be as loved if he had not been killed? Had he not been assassinated, Kennedy would have turned 90 in the spring of 2007, and one can only guess at whether he would still have been revered. Instead, he died at the age of 46, and Americans who lived at that time kept a permanent image of Kennedy as the president who died too young, the family man who was mourned, and the president who had inspired many young baby boomers to pursue public service in volunteer organizations such as the Peace Corps.

five years. War always falls hardest on the young, and the baby boomers marched off to a war that many of them did not understand and found increasingly pointless. Their fathers had fought in a ghastly, but necessary, war, against Germany, Italy, and Japan. However, in the case of the Vietnam War there seemed to be no imminent threat to the United States or to democracy, and many young Americans began to turn against the war.

Baby boomers were divided about the war in Vietnam. Although many were proud to serve their country, many others were increasingly disturbed about the lack of progress in the war. One cannot say that all baby boomers supported the war, or that all baby boomers were against it. The most vocal baby boomers, however, were those who, in ever-increasing numbers, protested against it.

In 1967, there developed what we would now call a perfect storm (an expression from the 1990s), one in which feminism, the desires of youth, and antiwar sentiment came together in a massive, prolonged discontent with the U.S. government. Never before, at least not since the time of the American Civil War, had Americans been so divided about a set of issues.

In November 1967, Dr. Benjamin Spock and four others were indicted for counseling young men about how to avoid the military draft. The New Haven Five were placed on trial in the beginning of 1968, and Dr. Spock was suddenly in the headlines once more. Millions of American parents, who had been much younger when they first purchased *Baby and Child Care*, remembered him and quite a few criticized him about what had happened to American youth during the 20 years since his book had been published.

BLAMING SPOCK

At the height of this youthful discontent, *Newsweek* ran a cover story entitled "Bringing Up Baby," in September 1968. The cover showed an infant holding a flower, a symbol of the youth and peace movements. The baby's sweater had a number of buttons, with slogans such as "Kindergarten Power," "The Permission Society," and "Don't Trust Anyone Over 7," an obvious reference to the general belief among American youth that no one over the age of 30 could be trusted. In the interest of full disclosure, *Newsweek* announced that medical editor Matt Clark, one of the writers of the story, had been a patient of Dr. Spock back in the 1930s, before Spock wrote *Baby and Child Care*! The article described the new generation that Spock helped to create:

During the late 1960s, pediatrician Benjamin Spock came under fire for his revolutionary childrearing techniques, which many Americans believed had helped create a society in which young people thought it was OK to defy their elders. Here, Spock (second from the left) marches with Dr. Martin Luther King Jr. (center) in an anti-Vietnam War rally in New York City's Central Park on April 15, 1967.

On the most superficial level, they wear their hair too long and their skirts too short and play their transistors too loud. Worse, some smoke pot and use obscene language. But of all the insults that the young inflict upon adult society, perhaps the most galling is that they systematically thumb their noses at authority—at the values of their parents, the precepts of their teachers and the actions of their governments.[13]

Since Spock had been arrested and indicted, a number of leading social critics had assailed him for helping to create the "Permission Society," which allowed young people to defy their elders and consume the nation in protest and conflict. Dr. Norman Vincent Peale, who had written *The Power of Positive Thinking*, one of the first self-help books, summed up Spock's notions of child care as "Feed 'em whatever they want, don't let them cy, instant gratification of needs." [14] *Newsweek* went on to say that the youth culture that was inundating the United States was having a major impact elsewhere, and that British, French, German, and Danish adolescents were acting in a similar fashion. Spock answered his critics in the *Newsweek* article, saying

> I admit there are problems. But when Norman Vincent Peale accuses me of helping parents raise spoiled children, I say nonsense. I didn't have that much influence. Besides, he's not talking about spoiled kids, he's talking about activists who are against discrimination. Compared with the kids of the 1950s I think they're wonderful. I would be proud to say I helped encourage liberal parents to understand their kids. [15]

At the end of the 1960s, it was apparent that American society had changed radically during the past decade. American girls and women now wanted to be equal in all ways to boys and men. A serious generation gap existed between parents who had come of age during World War II and children who had grown up in the Sixties. As a result, traditional sources of wisdom and guidance, whether from church, the community, or family, seemed to have much less influence than before.

These issues would not go away in the 1970s, but they would be reshaped and redefined by a number of things, including Supreme Court decisions, influential books, and even by television shows.

4

All in the Family

Despite what 1960s activists sometimes said, no one ever outgrows the desire to have a family. Commitment to and support from a group is a basic human need. The ways in which that need could be met, and the shape of families themselves, were tested and retested during the 1970s.

A NEW VOICE

In 1970, *Dare to Discipline*, written by Dr. James Dobson of southern California, was an answer to the theories of Dr. Spock and a challenge to the permissive society that so many social critics believed had taken over the United States. Born in Louisiana in 1936, Dobson was not a baby boomer, but his life and career had unfolded in ways that would have made a baby boomer proud. An overachiever from an early age and the son of a Protestant minister, Dobson decided that education and family matters, rather than religion, would be his focus. When Tyndale House Publishers released *Dare to Discipline*, they unveiled a new voice to the masses, one that spoke of firmness and certainty on the part of parents:

> Have you considered the fact that the present generation of young people [baby boomers] has enjoyed more of the "good life" than any comparable group in the history of the world? One can define the good life any way he chooses; the conclusion

remains the same. Our children have had more pleasure and entertainment, better food, more leisure time, better education, better medicine, more material goods, and more opportunities than has ever been known before. Yet they have been described as the "angry generation."[16]

It was hard to argue with these facts. Those born after 1945 had enjoyed more advantages than any previous American generation. Why were they so angry? Dobson offered this explanation:

> Most of the popular answers are essentially wrong. The conflict has not occurred because of hypocrisy in the older generation. There has always been hypocrisy in human society and it is certainly well represented in ours. But if hypocrisy is the root-cause of the turmoil, why didn't previous generations respond as violently? Something else is operating now . . . the central cause of the turmoil among the young must again be found in the tender years of childhood: we demanded neither respect nor responsible behavior from our citizens, and it should not be surprising that some of our young citizens are now demonstrating the absence of these virtues.[17]

Dobson argued that discipline was as important as love. That seems self-evident in some respects but, if he was correct, American parents had gone overboard on the latter and neglected the former. While he admitted that discipline could be overdone and that there were indeed horror stories of children who were abused, Dobson asserted that the great problem of the time ran counter to this belief: Too many children manipulated, and sometimes even terrorized, their parents. He gave one poignant example after another of how permissive parents had found that their all-consuming love had backfired. Their children were disrespectful as kids, surly as teenagers, and even worse as young adults. Without mentioning Dr. Spock by name, Dobson railed against the attitude that it was enough to "(1) raise the child in an atmosphere of genuine affection; (2) satisfy his material and physical needs."[18]

Dobson later confided that the turning point in his life, the moment when he knew he must act, came in April 1966, when *Time* ran a cover story with the question "Is God Dead?" Dobson believed that morals and ethics in society derived from good parenting, which was itself informed by a respect for, and perhaps a fear of, God. Admission of such a belief might have thwarted the sales of some books, but Dobson found his audience: *Dare to Discipline* sold more than 3 million copies between 1970 and 2000. As he became the voice for a new morality that was founded upon the old morality, Dobson and his followers were confronted with another challenge.

ROE V. WADE

In January 1973, the Supreme Court ruled in *Roe v. Wade*, a landmark decision that struck down most attempts by states to outlaw abortion. Until then, the matter had been largely in the hands of the individual states; now it had become a matter for the federal government. The Supreme Court declared that women had a right to privacy, which included the right to have an abortion. Seldom has any one decision by the Supreme Court had so great an impact on American life.

In the five years that followed *Roe v. Wade*, Americans of all backgrounds and religions found a new way to differentiate themselves, becoming known either as *pro-life*, which meant "against abortion," or *pro-choice*, which meant "in favor of a woman's right to choose." Priests and pastors had immediately seen the positive or negative impact of the Supreme Court decision, but few politicians in 1973 realized how much the debate about abortion would shape Republican and Democratic party politics during the next 20 years.

THIRTY-FIVE CENTS   APRIL 8, 1966

TIME

THE WEEKLY NEWSMAGAZINE

Is God Dead?

VOL. 87 NO. 14

The April 8, 1966, cover of *Time* illustrated what many Americans thought was a general movement away from God and the religion-based values that had defined America in the past. In response, Evangelical Christians such as Dr. James Dobson formed a counter-movement that supported a Christian-based upbringing for children.

TELEVISION

In the 20 years between television's first appearance around 1950 and 1970, it had been noticeably staid; the programs produced reinforced a traditional way of looking at families.

Whether it was *Leave It to Beaver*, *My Three Sons*, *Ozzie and Harriet*, or *The Brady Bunch*, television programs seemed to suggest that the American family was staying together, even when the rest of the world was falling apart. That changed in the 1970s, leading to the point where social critics often claimed that television was accelerating the destruction of traditional values.

The giant in the field was CBS's *All in the Family*. First appearing in the winter of 1971, *All in the Family* had a nine-year run, during which the show explored controversies on virtually every aspect of American family life. Starring Carroll O'Connor as the irascible Archie Bunker and Jean Stapleton as his sweet and silly wife, Edith Bunker, the program poked fun at traditional values and the idea that these values could somehow return to prominence. The show's opening song, sung by O'Connor and Stapleton, lamented the loss of what had once been a more "normal" life in America.

All in the Family featured a running battle between conservative, blue-collar Archie Bunker and his son-in-law, Michael Stivic, a liberal, aspiring white-collar worker. Archie often assailed his son-in-law as "the Meathead," and Michael returned the favor by condemning Archie as a died-in-the-wool chauvinist pig. Neither character was truly likable, but the vitriol that passed between them suggested that the program's producers supported Stivic's point of view. Although relations between Edith Bunker and her daughter, Gloria Stivic, were much better, Edith often seemed at a loss when she tried to understand her daughter's choices and attitudes. Didn't she want to live like her mother and father? Didn't she believe in the values of an earlier time?

At its best, *All in the Family* served as a major sounding board for Americans on different positions concerning family values. Did a woman have the right to an abortion? Did a man have to support his family? Should affirmative

THE WALTONS—COUNTER TO ALL IN THE FAMILY

The Waltons ran on CBS for almost the same period as *All in the Family*, nine seasons. During those years one of the most familiar and comforting of television sounds was hearing "Good night, John boy," "Good night, Daddy," and the like.

Airing from 1972 to 1981, *The Waltons* was about life in rural Virginia during the Great Depression of the 1930s. The Waltons were a truly three-generational family, with Grandma and Grandpa, Momma and Daddy, and seven children. Each one-hour episode revolved around some important family or neighborhood concern, ranging from the important to the sublime; there was nothing trivial about *The Waltons*.

This was the kind of show critics might be expected to hate because of its emphasis on goody-goody characters, but few ever took it to task. There was something truly disarming, warming, and engaging about *The Waltons*: There were times when viewers yearned for the idyllic life of the 1930s, when the family gathered in the living room to listen to the president on the radio and each family member helped out around the house.

Forty years had passed since the events of the Great Depression and the reenactment shown on *The Waltons*, yet Americans of all ages watched the program. For senior citizens, *The Waltons* brought back sentimental, and sometimes painful, memories, while for young people it evoked an age that had disappeared, but that seemed to be recreated every Thursday night.

To the extent that *All in the Family* showed what the American family had become in the 1970s, *The Waltons* showed what it had been like in the 1930s. Of course, there were inconsistencies and inaccuracies; most depression-era families did not live as well or as comfortably as the Waltons, and most 1970s families did not argue as much as Archie and Michael did on *All in the Family*. Those who watched those programs in the 1970s came away with a feeling that the 1970s was, in many ways, television's golden age: A time when it came close to achieving some of the positive goals that it had set out to accomplish when it first appeared in the 1950s.

action programs, created in the 1960s, grant preferential treatment to blacks and other racial minorities? The show offered no easy answers; instead, it held up the problems and conflicts for all to see.

Many similar programs followed *All in the Family*, including *Maude* and *The Jeffersons*, but none was truly successful at imitating this influential program. *All in the Family* ran from 1971 to 1979, when *Archie Bunker's Place*, a tamer spin-off, replaced it.

YEAR OF THE EVANGELICAL

The Vietnam War finally ended in April 1975, when South Vietnam collapsed and fell. Thousands of U.S. soldiers and their Vietnamese allies were airlifted from Saigon just before its surrender. Americans were still divided about the war: Some said it had been a terrible disaster, while others claimed it had been a necessary sacrifice. For the most part, Americans were pleased to see the end of a conflict that had drained the U.S. Treasury and claimed 58,000 American lives. Many commentators and pundits believed that the presidential election of 1976 would focus on the failure in Vietnam, but this proved not to be the case. Instead, the 1976 election mostly revolved around matters of moral values.

James Earl Carter Jr., better known as Jimmy, emerged as the Democratic candidate by May 1976. Born and raised in Plains, Georgia, he was the first man from the Deep South to win the nomination of a major political party since before the Civil War. Carter was charming and famous for his smile, and he seemed to represent a return to earlier, simpler American values. Raised in a Baptist household, he had become a born-again Christian in the 1960s and was one of the most openly religious men ever to win the nomination of a major party.

Carter made an effort to show that he was not a throwback to earlier, simplistic times. He was the first presidential candidate to grant an interview to *Playboy*, where he revealed that he had experienced lust many times in his heart, but that he had refrained from acting upon it. Previous candidates had not felt it necessary to make this kind of statement. Although he was a born-again Christian, Carter was clearly pro-choice, and he was in favor of the Equal Rights Amendment (ERA), then pending the approval of the states.

Carter narrowly won the November 1976 election over Republican incumbent Gerald Ford, thereby becoming the first avowed born-again Christian to be elected in the twentieth century. *Time* dubbed 1976 the "Year of the Evangelical," and many other periodicals gave attention to this new phenomenon known as the Born Again movement. Suddenly, it seemed, millions of Americans were rediscovering their faith.

A BAPTIST IN THE WHITE HOUSE

Throughout American history, presidents had mostly come from the mainstrean Protestant groups such as the Congregational, Presbyterian, and Episcopal churches. (John F. Kennedy, a Catholic, had been the one major exception.) Jimmy Carter represented something different, coming from a Deep Southern tradition of the Baptist Church. These second-line, as opposed to mainline, Protestant denominations gained strength throughout the 1970s. Attendance at the mainline churches remained flat or even declined, while there was an increase in the number of charismatic, Pentecostal, and evangelical churches. (The era of the mega-church had not yet arrived; please see Chapter 9.) It is difficult to pinpoint the precise differences between charismatic, Pentecostal, and evangelical beliefs, but here is the explanation of former president Carter, written many years after he left office:

JIMMY CARTER & WALTER MONDALE

LEADERS, FOR A CHANGE.

VOTE DEMOCRATIC NOVEMBER 2ND

Paid for and authorized by 1976 Democratic Presidential Campaign Committee, Inc.

A self-defined born-again Christian, President Jimmy Carter represented the phenomenon of religiosity that was sweeping the United States in the mid-1970s. Like many Americans at the time, Carter openly displayed his Christian beliefs. Carter is pictured here with his running mate Walter Mondale on a campaign leaflet prior to the 1976 presidential election.

I consider the two primary meanings (Random House Dictionary of the English language) to be quite adequate: (a) "belonging to or designating Christian churches that emphasize the teachings and authority of the scriptures, especially of the New Testament, in opposition to the institutional authority of the church itself, and that stress as paramount the tenet that salvation is achieved by personal conversion to faith in the atonement of Christ," or (b) "designating Christians, especially of the late 1970s, eschewing the designation of fundamentalist but holding to a conservative interpretation of the Bible."[19]

The key distinction was between the words *fundamentalist* and *evangelical*. A fundamentalist Christian, a term coined in the 1920s, refers to someone who strictly followed the words of the Old and New Testaments. Evangelical Christians hold similar beliefs but did not want to be called fundamentalist, which had negative associations with the Scopes Monkey Trial of 1925. President Carter was definitely an evangelical Christian, but he was not a fundamentalist. Given that evangelical Christian churches were on the rise during the 1970s, one would expect Carter to enjoy a strong base of popularity throughout his presidency, but this was not the case, for he ran afoul of a newly resurgent fundamentalist movement.

Carter's Troubles

Carter ran into trouble almost from the start. Although he never needed the kind of trappings that Richard Nixon had, and this lack of vanity was refreshing to Americans. But Carter faced a rising sea of problems. America, it seemed, truly was as divided as *All in the Family* suggested. Millions of Americans thought the women's liberation movement had been good but that it was insufficient. They believed it necessary to have a children's movement; a gay, lesbian, and bisexual movement; and perhaps some others, as well.

On the other side, millions of Americans felt, perhaps like Archie Bunker, that the women's liberation movement had been bad enough, and that no more should be tolerated.

If anyone could have found his way through this cultural divide, it should have been the plainspoken man from Plains, Georgia, who followed a strong personal morality. But Carter proved unable to juggle the demands of his different constituencies. Although he was a Southern Baptist, Carter had become a follower of the women's liberation movement, and by 1979, the year he called for the White House Conference on Families, he had been branded a traitor to the cause of traditional, white men.

Carter had spoken of the need for a White House conference as early as 1976, but it did not convene until June 1980; even then, it met in Baltimore, Maryland, rather than in Washington, D.C. Carter addressed the delegates: "I want the conference to be a catalyst for a new awareness in the government which I head. . . . Where government is helpful to families, let it be strengthened. Where government is harmful to families, let it be changed. . . . I will do all I can to ensure that your work does not end just as a report on the shelves in Washington."[20]

The conference engendered a good deal of soul-searching on the part of more than 2,000 delegates, but there was controversy, as well. A few hundred marched out of the conference during the first and second day, convinced that it would be nothing more than a sound piece for the gay-lesbian-bisexual agenda. Most delegates were in their thirties and forties, and they tended to bring a fairly liberal tone to the proceedings, but there were some exceptions. Dr. James Dobson, who had written *Dare to Discipline* a decade earlier, came to the conference to warn the federal government to stay clear of family matters, suggesting that the federal government would only complicate matters. He voiced a strong objection to the Domestic Violence and Treatment Act, saying that the federal government should not interfere in disputes between husbands and wives.

Dr. Tamara Hareven, a professor of history, sounded a very different note when she sought to refute the idea that there had previously been a golden age for American families. Rather than three generations who lived peacefully under one roof, she said, Americans had almost always lived in nuclear families, partly because the grandparents had died younger in earlier times. Hareven pointed out that there had always been stresses and strains on family relationship, and said about the prevalence of divorce in 1970s America:

> In the nineteenth century people did not resort to divorce as frequently as they do now, because divorce was considered socially unacceptable. This does not mean, however, that families were living happily and in harmony. A high rate of desertion and separation of couples replaced legal divorce. And those couples which did not resort to divorce or separation despite their incompatibility lived together as strangers, in deep conflict. Thus, the increase in divorce statistics, as such, is no proof of family breakdown.[21]

The White House Conference on Families made a number of specific recommendations as to how the federal government could improve the lives of working families. One such measure was to change the so-called Marriage Penalty, which showed that a married couple paid more in federal tax than if they had chosen to file as two separate individuals. The general consensus among the delegates who had chosen to remain at the conference was that the definition of family needed to be broadened. American family life had changed so much in the preceeding two decades that one could no longer assume it referred to the traditional, nuclear family with complete certainty.

The delegates who stayed for the entire conference adjourned after three days, with high hopes and prospects for the future. They did not realize that the 300 delegates who had walked out were more in step with the nation than they were, and they did not anticipate the vehemence with which traditional family and cultural values would reassert themselves over the next eight years.

5

Ronald Reagan and the Christian Right

Most photographs of Ronald Reagan show a fine-looking man with a sunny disposition in the autumn years of his life, yet filled with an elastic type of vitality. How did this former movie actor and California governor become identified with conservative American values? More important, how did he forge such an important alliance with an assortment of groups that has been bunched together and labeled "the Christian Right?"

BIRTH OF THE CHRISTIAN RIGHT

Even today, many years after the fact, it is difficult to say just when and where the Christian Right was born. Most scholars agree that it happened in the late 1970s in response to a series of Supreme Court Decisions, including *Roe v. Wade*, with a special emphasis on the year 1979, but few can be more precise than that. One fact is certain: The Christian Right was formed in response to what was considered the moral, political, and economic malaise of the United States during the Carter administration of 1977 to 1981.

President Carter spoke of the malaise in a televised address to the nation in the summer of 1979. Prices, especially of oil, were rising and wages were falling. The American family was splintered between baby boomers in their early thirties and their parents, who were still functioning in their sixties. People questioned how the new generation should be raised, but there was no Dr. Spock to guide the way. If one single event can be the symbol for everything that went wrong in the late 1970s, it was the failure to address a national humiliation, which began when militant Iranian university students seized the U.S. Embassy in Tehran on November 4, 1979.

Americans had faced international crises before, but none that had left the country in such a weak and divided state. President Carter seemed unable to coerce the Iranian government, which claimed it was unable to police its university students. As the days passed, with no end in sight, the Iran hostage crisis became the defining event of 1979, 1980, and almost 1981, as well.

In April 1980, President Carter finally authorized a dramatic attempt to free the hostages, but the effort failed. U.S. helicopters were grounded in Iranian sand and five members of the U.S. Air Forece and three U.S. Marines were killed during the rescue attempt. No hostages were freed. This was a painful sight to Americans of the World War II generation; the knowledge that Israel had been so much more successful in recent hostage rescues, such as the dramatic rescue of more than 100 people in Uganda in 1976, made them feel even worse. In June 1980, as President Carter convened the White House Conference on Families, Americans felt a sense of dread, perhaps even doom, about their place in the world.

ENTER REAGAN

Born in 1911 in Illinois, Ronald Reagan was no baby boomer. Throughout a life in the public eye, he stood very much for the values and attitudes of the baby boomer's parents. He started his career in radio and then appeared in a number

FATHERS AND DAUGHTERS

One of the most peculiar scenes from public life in the 1980s involved conflict between prominent fathers and their activist daughters. The most famous, or infamous, case was that of Ronald Reagan and Patti Davis, but there were a number of others, including Henry Fonda and Jane Fonda.

As Reagan swept into the presidency in 1980, few knew much about his relationship with his daughter Patti, but her side of the story was about to become headline news. Born in 1952, the elder child of Reagan's second marriage, Patti Davis (she intentionally used her mother's maiden name) eventually revealed that she had been beaten by her mother and emotionally neglected by her father, whom she described as an affable, out-to-lunch kind of parent. Her autobiography was not published until after her father's presidency was over, but it came as a real shock to many who thought he had stood for family values. Patti Davis posed for *Playboy* in 1994, leading to further polarization in the public mind.

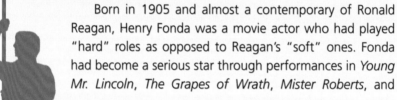

Born in 1905 and almost a contemporary of Ronald Reagan, Henry Fonda was a movie actor who had played "hard" roles as opposed to Reagan's "soft" ones. Fonda had become a serious star through performances in *Young Mr. Lincoln*, *The Grapes of Wrath*, *Mister Roberts*, and

of B movies. He then became the national spokesman for the General Electric Company in the 1950s, a part he filled to perfection. He had been a New Deal Democrat and a supporter of President Franklin D. Roosevelt earlier in life, but Reagan became a conservative by about the age of 40. By the time he was in his fifties, he had become a spokesman for the conservative movement. Although he seldom spoke about family values, Reagan often seemed to act the part; his on-air spots for General Electric often showcased his relationship with his wife, Nancy, and their two young children, Patti and Ron. It was less widely known that he had a daughter Maureen and a son Michael from his previous marriage to actress Jane Wyman.

12 Angry Men. Millions of viewers had come to believe in the man behind the performances: Fonda appeared to be the model of the self-made American who stuck to his guns, his virtue, and his values no matter what the cost.

What a shock it was when his actress daughter Jane Fonda revealed herself as a liberal political activist in the 1960s. She gained notoriety for being a sex symbol in the 1968 movie *Barbarella* and seemed like a typical child of the Sixties. Fans of her father forgave her until she went to North Vietnam in 1971 to show solidarity with the Communist government of that nation. From that moment on, she was branded as "Hanoi Jane," a label she would never shake.

In 1981, Henry Fonda and his daughter starred together in *On Golden Pond*, considered one of the best films of that year, and perhaps of the decade. The crusty old traditional father and his aging liberal daughter traded barbs as well as hugs in a movie that seemed as real as it was invented, as passionate as it was political. Family values had come a long way since Henry Fonda had made his big films in the 1930s, but he and his daughter showed some signs of bridging the generation gap that had developed during the 1960s. Henry Fonda died in 1982.

Reagan entered politics in the 1960s, first becoming governor of California, then a candidate for the nation's highest office. He lost a close race against incumbent Gerald Ford for the 1976 Republican nomination, and in 1980, he was back for another run. Active and spry at 69, Reagan seemed like the perfect Republican answer to Democrat Jimmy Carter, even though some of Reagan's opponents in the Republican primaries lambasted his economic theories, one of them calling them "voodoo economics." When he was nominated, in July 1980, Reagan already had a good chance to win, but he was about to be helped by another constituency, one he knew little about. The Christian Right was about to sweep Reagan and a number of other prominent Republicans into office.

Thanks to the backing of the Christian Right, former actor Ronald Reagan received the Republican nomination for president in 1980. Reagan is pictured here at his ranch near Santa Barbara, California, the summer before he defeated Jimmy Carter in the 1980 presidential election.

MORAL MAJORITY INC.

In the summer of 1979, even before the start of the Iran Hostage Crisis, a handful of leading conservatives gathered to found a new movement, which they called Moral Majority Inc. Although none of them claimed to have received inspiration from Archie Bunker or from *All in the Family*, they raised concerns that echoed those of the blue-collar worker on the television program. What had happened to America? How had the permissive society, as they called it, come to replace Mom, apple pie, and the American flag? What could be done?

The premise behind Moral Majority was that Americans actually *were* a traditionalist people who revered the flag, the nation, and its place in the world, and who preferred the traditional nuclear family to nontraditional ones. Moral Majority leader Jerry Falwell (see sidebar on page 56) argued that his movement did not need to create a new belief in American values; it had only to rekindle the belief that already existed.

THE PARTY PLATFORMS

The party platforms of 1980 showed that the Republican Party had moved to the right and the Democratic Party had moved to the left rather than closer to the center. As recently as 1976, many Republicans had quietly accepted the idea that a woman had the right to choose whether or not to have an abortion. In 1980, however, the Republican platform endorsed a right-to-life mindset, assailing Democratic policies regarding the traditional American family: "The family is the foundation of our social order. It is the school of democracy. . . . But the Democrats have shunted the family aside. They have given its power to the bureaucracy, its jurisdiction to the courts, and its resources to government grantors. For the first time in our history, there is real concern that the family may not survive."[22]

The Democratic Party shot back: "While the American family structure has changed radically in recent years, the family remains the key unit of our society. . . . Government cannot and should not attempt to displace the responsibilities of the family; to the contrary, the challenge is to formulate policies which will strengthen the family."[23]

THE ELECTION OF 1980

Carter and Reagan had very different campaign styles. Carter emphasized America's threatened position in the world, urging Americans to worry, while Reagan focused on America's great potential for good, both at home and abroad. Even voters who shared many of the same beliefs as Carter, found themselves turning to Reagan because of his bravado.

Reagan proved adroit at courting the Christian evangelical vote. In August 1980, he addressed the Religious Roundtable in Dallas, Texas, saying:

> When I hear the First Amendment used as a reason to keep traditional moral values away from policymaking, I am shocked. The First Amendment was written not to protect the people and the laws from religious values, but to protect those values from government tyranny. But over the last two or three decades the Federal Government seems to have forgotten both "that old time religion" and that old time Constitution.[24]

Reagan went on to say that he did not expect the Christian leaders to back him explicitly, but that "I want you to know I endorse you and what you are doing."[25]

The leadership of both the Republican and Democratic parties had spoken mostly about secular values for the past 20 years, so it came as a real surprise to hear Reagan solicit the *New Religious Right*, a term coined around that time by Martin E. Marty, professor of theology at the University of Chicago. In the presidential debates that followed, Reagan and Carter spoke more of secular problems such as oil, Iran, and the Soviet Union than of religious ones, but Reagan's appearance at the Religious Roundtable lit a fire under

One of Ronald Reagan's biggest supporters during his presidential campaign in 1980 was Reverend Jerry Falwell. The cofounder of the Moral Majority is pictured here with Reagan during a campaign stop in Lynchburg, Virginia, in October 1980.

evangelical Christian leaders. *Newsweek* ran a cover story on "Born-Again Politics" that showed Jerry Falwell inside an image of a cross, which served as the letter "t" in the word "Vote." Liberal columnist Meg Greenfield commented on how Reagan's alliance with the New Christian Right had changed the face of American politics:

> The evangelicals are coming. Not since Genghis Khan rode west, we are informed, has anything so ominous been in prospect. These are said to be the values-police, the would-be enforcers of rigid, outmoded morality, an unenlightened, vengeful, churchy crew that has worked its will on the Republicans' platform and is now propelling Ronald Reagan into office.[26]

JERRY FALWELL: COFOUNDER OF THE MORAL MAJORITY

Reviled as a demon by some and beloved by many others, Jerry Falwell was one of the most controversial of all American leaders in the 1970s and 1980s.

Born in Lynchburg, Virginia, in 1933, Falwell had a rather unstable childhood, as he later described to one of his biographers. His father killed his uncle in a fight in a local bar, and Falwell grew up in a community that felt assailed by the rising strength of secular values.

After Bible college in the Midwest, Falwell came home, and within a few years he started his own church in Lynchburg. Employing a vigorous speaking style, he developed a radio ministry a few years later, and by the 1970s, his "The Old Time Gospel Hour" was one of the most popular and successful of all radio programs. Originally, Falwell did not think he or other ministers should enter politics, but the battles against abortion and the Equal Rights Amendment brought him into the national spotlight. By 1979, he had become the most visible leader of what observers began to call the New Christian Right, to distinguish it from the Old Christian Right of the 1910s and 1920s.

In the winter of 1979, Falwell was approached by a small number of businessmen and church leaders, asking him to become the leader of a new organization. Dubbed Moral Majority Inc., the new group called for Christian morality in government, Christian values in the home, and a rejection of secularism.

"Moral Majority" proved to be a poor name choice. Opponents on the left carried bumper stickers that read "The Moral Majority is neither." Falwell had considerable success in the early 1980s, however, claiming that Moral Majority had helped to unseat a number of leading secular liberals from public office.

Falwell ran into financial difficulties in the late 1980s, and Moral Majority Inc. was disbanded, only to be replaced by the Christian Coalition of America. Falwell continued to be enormously popular in the Christian evangelical community, which accurately perceived him to be one of the most outspoken and fearless leaders of its cause. Falwell died in May 2007 at age 73.

Election Day confirmed what many had suspected. Ronald Reagan rode a powerful wave into office. Although Reagan captured only 51 percent of the total vote, he came out with nearly 10 percent more of the popular vote than Jimmy Carter, in part because Independent candidate John Anderson won 6.6 percent of the popular vote. Reagan ended up winning 44 out of 50 states. Just as important, a number of prominent secular Democratic liberals such as George McGovern, Frank Church, and others lost their Senate seats in what seemed like a Republican whirlwind.

REAGAN IN OFFICE

It must be said that Reagan was a disappointment to the Christian Right. Although they thought him far better than Carter or any other Democrat, they found Reagan to deliver very little in terms of family values.

Reagan appointed almost no major leaders of the Christian Right to public office during his administration, and there were certainly no prominent members of that group in his cabinet. Reagan proved far more interested in economic issues than in social ones, and here he did lend his support, in a rather half-hearted way, to the Christian Right.

Under Reagan, it became more difficult to receive welfare benefits. The federal government sought to return as much power, especially in fiscal matters, as possible to the states. At the same time, the federal budget ballooned, in part because of Reagan's insistence on a strong defense, to be used as a deterrent against aggression by the Soviet Union. In the first two years of Reagan's administration, many social programs were slashed while the military budget grew rapidly. This did not bother most of Reagan's supporters on the Christian Right, for they had said all along that families could take better care of themselves than the government could. Still, there were rumblings of discontent from the religious right. Was the avowedly conservative Reagan that much of an improvement over the self-declared liberal Jimmy Carter?

Only in one area did cultural conservatives really win the day. Ever since Betty Friedan had first penned *The Feminine Mystique*, there had been agitation for an amendment to the Constitution to declare the equal rights of women under the law. This movement had created the Equal Rights Amendment (ERA), passed by both houses of Congress in 1972. However, the ERA had stalled in its attempt to be passed by two-thirds of the states. As recently as 1977, it had seemed only a matter of time before the ERA would win approval, but cultural conservatives, led by Phyllis Schlafly, had mobilized a powerful response.

Why, asked Schlafly, should women forgo the special treatment they now receive from men? Why should they seek equality before the law when they already enjoy superior treatment under the culture? Schlafly proved adept at manipulating and even frightening state legislators, and in June 1982, the ERA came to a dead end, just three states short of the two-thirds majority needed. Although many feminists and liberals spoke of trying again, the failure to pass the ERA sent a message: The country seemed to have become more conservative.

6

The Pursuit of Pleasure

One of the strongest and most lasting public images of the 1980s involves hypocrisy. It was a time, critics said, when the rich got richer on the backs of the poor. It was a time when conservatives ran the government, but they ran up the federal budget deficit. Perhaps most important, it was a time when preachers scolded and berated their parishioners, only to be found guilty of immorality.

RISE OF THE YUPPIES

The dictionary defines *yuppies* as "young urban professionals." This definition first appeared in 1983, about the time that Ronald Reagan's administration had firmly changed the direction of the nation's priorities, placing more of an emphasis on defense spending. One reason that made it easier for Reagan and his policy makers to create this shift was that it was apparent that many baby boomers were doing well economically, even quite well.

The oldest of the baby boomers turned 30 in 1976, the year the nation celebrated its bicentennial, and they turned 35 the year Ronald Reagan took office. It was not unusual that they suddenly gained economic prominence; for generations, 35 had been something of a magic number as far as earning power and economic status were concerned. The oldest of the baby boomers, and their slightly younger brothers and sisters who were born during the next five years, though, seemed much more interested in flaunting their wealth than had past generations.

Only 20 years before, it had been seen as gauche and immature to show off one's wealth. "Old" money had been distinguished from "new" money by the way it was gracefully concealed, and many a millionaire had managed to come across as just another middle- or working-class guy. The early- to mid-1980s was a period when this type of behavior was rejected and material goods were embraced. In other words, if you had wealth, flaunt it.

Young urban professionals had money because they had entered the right professions at the right time. Aspiring young lawyers and businessmen had plenty of cash on hand, and they often put off having children, which was reflected in the declining birthrates throughout the 1970s. As a result, many yuppies lived in magnificent town houses near the big cities and sometimes acquired fine country homes as well. A term closely associated with yuppie, *DINK*, also appeared in the national vocabulary. It meant "Double income, no kids."

Many upper-middle-class Americans built much larger homes than ever before, which reflected their personal wealth. The author of *Sex and Real Estate: Why We Love Houses*, put it this way:

> Have you ever noticed that there are usually *no people* in the luscious layouts of these magazines? The overstuffed couch, the Persian rug, the grassy lane, the inglenook with the nautical view—all are empty, available, inviting. . . . Besides, adds Ingrid Sischy of *Interview*, "pictures of hubby and the wife" now look "old-fashioned" since family structures have changed. Children, "less old-fashioned" as accessories, make occasional cameo appearances along with the more usual pugs and whippets, but the overwhelming majority of magazines still prefer the allure

of the perfectly set table and the deliciously furnished, temptingly empty room.[27]

Of course, this type of expansive and largely empty living was not a reflection of the average American family home. Only the very top of the baby boomer class, those making more than $100,000 a year in the mid-1980s, could even aspire to this way of living. This way of living, though, particularly the emphasis on material possessions rather than people, became a goal to which many people quietly aspired. What can be said with some certainty is that the baby boomers had come of age, economically speaking, and that they wanted as much as they could get. Economists and sociologists of the mid-1980s agreed that: (1) middle-aged Americans wanted, and often had, more freedom than their parents had; (2) middle-class and upper-middle-class Americans now saw the family home as an investment, at least as much as a commitment to a place in which to raise children; (3) the suburbs had almost completely replaced the one-time working class communities close to the urban centers, and (4) America was splitting into a land of "haves" and "have-nots" with much of the difference determined by where one lived. There was another sign of the times, however: a return to religion.

REVIVAL RELIGION

Americans had long been a religious people; religious historians counted no less than three "Great Awakenings" of religious faith in the past. It is generally agreed that a fourth Great Awakening began in the 1960s and 1970s, rose to prominence in the 1980s, and came to an end in the 1990s. The most outstanding examples of this new religious revival tended to come from the South and Midwest, and bible-thumping preachers who sounded a bit like those of the 1920s often led the congregations.

By the time the last of the baby boomers came of age in the mid-1980s, many had achieved economic success, and thus a new term, *yuppie*, or young urban professional, was used to define them. Here, the May 19, 1986, issue of *Time* celebrates the boomers' 40th birthday party with a cake and memorabilia from the 1960s.

Mainstream American culture, which was often defined by *Time*, *Newsweek*, and the *New York Times*, had not paid attention to the religious revival, so Americans were astonished at the sudden appearance of so many large churches, which people began to call mega-churches, in the South and Midwest. Preachers whose fathers and grandfathers had to strain to be heard began to use microphones, loudspeakers, and even went on television as the new televangelists of the 1980s. Some of the biggest, loudest, and most successful were Jim and Tammy Bakker and Reverend Jimmy Swaggart.

Ronald Reagan was easily reelected in 1984. This time, the political debate revolved around taxes rather than family values; Reagan promised to lower taxes, while his Democratic opponent, Walter Mondale, suggested he might have to raise them. Evangelicals were again disappointed by the results, for Reagan appointed no leading Christian

Televangelists such as Reverend Jimmy Swaggart used television as a medium to spread their Christian beliefs to millions of people throughout the world. *The Jimmy Swaggart Telecast* was broadcast to approximately 200 television stations during its heyday in the mid-1980s. Here, audience members react to Swaggart's message during a rally in Milwaukee, Wisconsin, in February 1985.

PAT ROBERTSON: FOUNDER OF THE CHRISTIAN COALITION OF AMERICA

Pat Robertson had a soft smile and an easy way with words; some said he was as good a communicator as Ronald Reagan. Although he was one of the easiest of the evangelicals to underestimate, Pat Robertson was as devoted to the Christian cause as any man of his era.

Born in Virginia in 1930, Robertson was the son of Absalom Willis Robertson, a U.S. Representative who later became a U.S. Senator and who championed the cause of segregation in the 1950s. Raised more on politics than religion, Robertson graduated from Washington and Lee University and Yale Law School, spending some time in between to serve in the U.S. Marines. He had a born-again experience in his late 20s, entered divinity school, and first ministered to a poor black neighborhood in Brooklyn, New York. His real calling, however, was in the new medium of television.

Moving back to Virginia, Robertson founded the Christian Broadcast Network (CBN) in 1960. In 1966, he started a live televison show on CBN known as the 700 Club and became one of the best fund-raisers among the televangelists. One could almost say he had invented the craft. During the 1960s and 1970s he largely avoided

conservatives to his cabinet. Leaders like Pat Robertson and Jerry Falwell were deeply disappointed by Reagan's actions in office, but they continued to believe he was far superior to any Democrat who might emerge.

THE HORRIBLE YEAR

In addition to not appointing any members of the Christian Right to cabinet positions, Reagan sometimes seemed to drift, leaving policy matters in the hands of his very secular staff, headed by Secretary of the Treasury Donald Regan and White House Deputy Chief of Staff Michael discussing political issues, but by 1980 he had become one of the most expressive of all the televangelists. Like many of his followers, Robertson had supported Jimmy Carter's run for the presidency in 1976 and was disappointed with the results. In 1980 and 1984, he backed Ronald Reagan, but in 1988 he ran for the presidency himself.

With no prior political experience, Robertson came in a distant fourth in the Republican primaries, but even that was better than many had predicted. Undaunted, he soon founded the Christian Coalition of America, putting Ralph Reed in charge of day-to-day affairs. Robertson returned to CBN, where he was as outspoken and controversial as ever.

As anyone who has been in the public eye knows, it is easy to make mistakes. Robertson had been the head of the CBN for 40 years, when he stumbled badly in the fall of 2005. He suggested that the United States should "go ahead" and assassinate Venezuelan president Hugo Chavez. For many outside the evangelical fold, this was the denouement to Robertson's career, but to his eager and faithful followers, it was another indication that here was a man who could not be put in a box, and could not be forced to use the language of political correctness.

Deaver. By the middle of Reagan's second term, some on the Christian Right decided that if they were ever to have a real voice at the table, one of them would have to run for president. Not surprisingly, it was Pat Robertson who came forward.

Robertson gathered support during 1986 and planned to announce his bid to run for president at some point in 1987. The credibility of all television preachers, however, suddenly came under close scrutiny that spring, which has been known ever since as the time of "Holygate," "Holy War," or the "Time of Troubles" for the evangelical community.

On January 4, 1987, televangelist Oral Roberts made a startling speech in which he asked his parishioners, near and far, to send in $4.5 million in donations by March; otherwise, he might be "called home" by God. The naked appeal for money brought ridicule from the mainstream press, and Roberts was criticized on many fronts. The worst was still to come.

On March 19, 1987, Reverend Jim Bakker of the Praise The Lord Club (PTL) resigned his post, in the wake of reports of a sordid one-night stand with Jessica Hahn, a former church secretary. Worse, it was revealed that the PTL had paid more than a quarter of a million dollars to the woman and her lawyers to keep the incident quiet.

Fellow evangelicals denounced Bakker, who, with his wife Tammy, had formed the Jim and Tammy evangelical show. He was defrocked, and he later spent some time in prison for fraud, tax evasion, and racketeering.

Jerry Falwell stepped into the breach, accepting a new position as temporary leader of the PTL Club. Even Falwell, with his large base of support, found that the PTL was an albatross dragging down his own organization. Within two years, Falwell jettisoned the PTL and disbanded his own Moral Majority Inc. By this time, funds were running dry for most of the televangelists.

In May 1987, just two months after Jim Bakker had to step down, Democratic presidential candidate Gary Hart, a senator from Colorado, had to leave the presidential race after it was discovered that he had a tryst with Donna Rice, a young model aboard a yacht appropriately named *Monkey Business*. By the end of that tumultuous spring, both the evangelical community and American voters at large were amazed at the debauchery of so many individuals they had thought to be respectable.

ROBERTSON DECLARES

On October 4, 1987, Pat Robertson went to Bedford-Stuyvesant, a section of Brooklyn, where he had ministered during the early days of his career. Greeted by as many hecklers as supporters, he made a strong speech about the importance of family values and announced his candidacy for president of the United States. Just three days later, ABC's *Nightline* revealed that Robertson had married his wife in 1957, when she was pregnant, and that his eldest son was born only eleven weeks after the wedding. Robertson admitted to television reporters that he had followed the way of "wine, women, and song" in his youth,

In 1988, televangelist Pat Robertson challenged then-vice president George H. W. Bush for the Republican nomination for president. Robertson ran on a very conservative platform, hoping to ban pornography and reform the educational system. Robertson is pictured here campaigning in January 1988.

but he said those days were long behind him. The public seemed ready to forgive him, when yet another startling revelation was made.

JIMMY SWAGGART'S FALL

In February 1988, just about a year after the fall of Jim and Tammy Bakker, Reverend Jimmy Swaggart made an emotional departure from his ministry. Standing before a large crowd and speaking to a television audience that may have been in the millions, Swaggart admitted that he had sinned, and that it was time for him to step aside, at least temporarily. He did not mention the specific sin, but photographs showed him entering a New Orleans area motel with a prostitute. The woman emerged to claim that Swaggart was a sex-obsessed man, someone she would not want to have around her children.

Iconoclastic journalist Hunter S. Thompson directed his scorn at the year of disgrace that commenced with Jim Bakker and ended with Jimmy Swaggart: "How long, O Lord, how long? Are these TV preachers *all* degenerates? Are they wallowing and whooping with harlots whenever they're not on camera? Are they *all* thieves and charlatans and whoremongers?"[28]

Many liberal, conservative, and middle-of-the-road Americans were asking the same questions.

A THOUSAND POINTS OF LIGHT

Ronald Reagan served two full terms as president, the first chief executive to do so since Dwight Eisenhower. When Reagan left office in January 1989, the United States was much different from the nation of eight years before.

Reagan had achieved many of his goals. The federal government was less involved in the lives of the American people. The economy was robust, although the federal

1980s TELEVISION

Given that the 1980s was a decade when many televangelists revealed their hypocrisy and many Americans seemed to be overly materialistic, it is interesting to note that a number of television programs seemed to hearken back to earlier times. There was nothing like *All in the Family* during the 1980s; one wonders if such a program could have gained a loyal audience.

Instead, the American family was portrayed in much more innocuous programs, such as *Family Ties*, which debuted in 1982, and *The Cosby Show*, which first aired in 1984.

Actor Michael J. Fox played teenage Alex P. Keaton, a conservative son of liberal parents, in a definite attempt to contrast baby boomer parents with their children. A conservative in terms of economics and social policy, Alex nonetheless proved to be a typically self-indulgent teenager, and the program made much of the back-and-forth between his values and those of his parents. *Family Ties* was the second-most popular program on TV from 1985 through 1987, finishing behind yet another family program, *The Cosby Show*.

Comedian Bill Cosby played Dr. Cliff Huxtable, an African American obstetrician who lived with his family in Brooklyn, New York. His wife, Clair, was an attorney, and the children all appeared "well above average." Although many critics attacked the show, saying it was not representative of the African American experience, the program proved enormously popular, winning as many awards and as many first-place ratings as *All in the Family* had done in the 1970s.

Family Ties and *The Cosby Show* both portrayed a very different American family from the previous two decades. If there was conflict in the Keaton or Huxtable homes, it was managed by the parents, who were more like mediators than authority figures. The problems in the outside world did not often intrude on the comfortable lives of the characters. That two such programs were so popular in the 1980s suggests, but does not prove, that Americans were ready and willing to look at their family situations in a more relaxed light than before. *Family Ties* and *The Cosby Show* did not represent a return to the type of family portrayed in *Leave It to Beaver*, but they were a long way from *All in the Family*.

deficit continued to balloon. In terms of family values, however, Reagan's eight years had been a failure. Virtually no major policy initiatives had been directed toward the family, and almost no substantive legislation had come forth.

George H. W. Bush, who had been vice president under Ronald Reagan, ran for president in his own right in 1988. The debates between Bush and Democrat Michael Dukakis tended to revolve around matters of national security and defense, rather than family values. Bush, who easily won the election, seemed ready to turn over many aspects of the federal government to private hands. Bush believed that Americans needed to be more engaged in public service, and during his inaugural address he called for a thousand points of light, meaning anything from helping a neighbor in a snowstorm to donating money to the needy. Few argued with Bush's domestic policy, but many noticed that he looked backward rather than forward, to a time when American society had been less aggressive and competitive.

7

A Clash of Generations

By 1990, it was apparent to most Americans that a culture war was taking place between those who believed in the traditional values of the 1930s and 1940s and those who had grown up during the 1960s and 1970s. Both groups had grown older, it was true, and they were far from being rigid in their beliefs, but the conflicts that had once been called the generation gap were still there for all to see.

Another cultural and generational group was about to assert itself. So much attention had been paid to the baby boomers, those born between 1946 and 1964, that scant time and attention had been left to those born after 1964. This new group of Americans, sometimes called the 13th generation, or Generation X, was about to make itself seen and heard, if not heeded.

THE EARLY 1990s

A description of Generation X first appeared in *Time* in the summer of 1990:

> They have trouble making decisions. They would rather hike in the Himalayas than climb a corporate ladder. They have few heroes, no anthems, no style to call their own. They crave entertainment, but their attention span is as short as one zap of a TV dial. They hate yuppies, hippies, and druggies. They postpone marriage because they dread divorce. . . . What they hold dear are family life, loafers and mountain bikes. They

JULY 16, 1990

Should the West Help Gorbachev?

$2.50

TIME

twentysomething

Laid back, late blooming or just lost?
Overshadowed by the baby boomers,
America's next generation has a hard
act to follow.

Deemed "laid back," "late bloomers," and "cynics," Generation
X was first recognized by *Time* in its July 16, 1990, issue. Many
Gen Xers believed that the American dream was no longer a reality
and it showed in their ambivalence.

possess only a hazy sense of their own identity but a
monumental preoccupation with all the problems the
preceding generation will leave for them to fix. This is the
twentysomething generation.[29]

Generational stereotypes are easier to write about than to truly understand, but there was much truth in the *Time* essay. Young people in 1990, those aged 18 to 29, were very different from those who belonged to the baby boom; in fact, many people called them the baby busters. Just a few years younger than the baby boomers, Gen Xers were acutely aware of the social ills of the past 20 years. Approximately 40 percent were children of divorced parents, which is a statistic that would have provoked incredulous disbelief in baby-boom times. As *Time* put it, "They virtually reared themselves."[30]

Young adults of Generation X also had gloomy, even dismal, views of the future. Most were aware that it was much harder to achieve the American Dream, however one defined it, than in the past. The decade of the 1980s had seen large increases in the Gross National Product (GNP) and in the number of those considered to be part of the upper class, but the real wages of the average working men and women had stagnated or declined. At the same time, the price of owning a home was skyrocketing, especially in attractive suburban areas.

When it came to family values, Generation X was decidedly ambivalent. "[President] Ronald Reagan was around longer than some of my friends' fathers," said one Generation Xer. "My generation will be the family generation," said another. "I don't want my kids to go through what my parents put me through."[31]

Researchers found that Gen Xers were especially resentful of the concept of "quality time," which many of their parents believed in during the 1980s. Persuaded by lifestyle experts, parents believed that the quality of the time spent was more important than the quantity of the time. People argued that most of the time parents are with their children, they are not doing anything significant or fun. The idea of quality time allowed mothers and fathers to feel better about being absent for most of the day, while caregivers stayed with their children. As long as the parents had some time in which they could do important things with their family, all would be well, or so they thought. This turned out to be a false assumption, and resentment over the illusory benefits of quality time proved to be the biggest flash point between Gen Xers and their parents.

Given their cynicism, it was surprising to find that Gen Xers admired activism, although with a more international flavor than in the past. Some Gen Xers moved to Nepal for a year or two; others tried to help the poor in Africa. Generation X heroes were people who helped others, and who did so in an unassuming manner. This generation had no overwhelming heroes such as John F. Kennedy or Betty Friedan, at least not yet. In fact, one of the major differences between them and their parents was the assumption that race and gender were no longer compelling issues in American life: Gen Xers thought the civil rights movement and the feminist movement had both succeeded in their goals. No one quite phrased it this way, but it seemed as if Generation X believed in a combination of family values and international activism.

THEIR OWN WAR

Twentysomethings had just appeared on the stage when the Persian Gulf War began—the first major conflict that involved the United States since the Vietnam War. In August 1990, just three weeks after the *Time* essay was published, Iraq invaded neighboring Kuwait, which first led to UN sanctions against Iraq and, later, armed conflict.

American life had changed in so many ways since the Vietnam War that it was easy to overlook one of the most important changes of all: In 1973, the United States discontinued the draft and employed an all-volunteer army. The young American men, and increasing number of women, who went to Iraq were volunteers who had joined the armed forces in the months and years prior to the Gulf War, because there was no draft in 1990 or 1991. Perhaps as a result of this shift, the peace, or antiwar, demonstrations of 1991 did not get very far. Americans as a whole were interested in supporting the troops abroad, and although there were protests, they did not affect the momentum of the buildup to war.

The Persian Gulf War itself was a straightforward operation. After nearly a month of bombing, U.S. and British coalition forces easily defeated Saddam Hussein's Iraqi Army in a 100-hour campaign. Kuwait was soon freed, and the war ended as a jubilant U.S. military received praise from all around. Hussein remained in power, but his ability to threaten his neighbors and to endanger the supply of oil to the Western world was much impaired.

The return of thousands of veterans of the Gulf War, in the summer of 1991, was in marked contrast to those who had returned from Vietnam 20 years earlier. To many observers, it seemed as if a major generational wound had been healed. Unfortunately, it came too late for Vietnam veterans, many of whom had lived painful and disjointed lives since their return from Southeast Asia.

BABY BOOM VERSUS WORLD WAR II

The presidential election of 1992 turned out to be one of the most important in some time. Of course, every presidential election has consequences, but 1992 seemed bigger than most. It matched a classic baby boomer, Democrat Bill Clinton, who espoused a 1960s kind of values system, against a classic World War II generation man, incumbent president George H. W. Bush.

BONO AND U2

When *Time* published its essay on twentysomethings in 1990, it lamented that Generation X had yet to find a musical style of its own. The music of the late 1980s seemed tired, even drab, by 1960s standards, and sometimes it seemed as if the best that could be found was an old Beatles or Rolling Stones album. This prediction went astray, however, as Gen Xers found inspiration from one of the most successful of all rock-and-roll bands.

U2 is an Irish band, formed in 1976. It burst onto the music scene in the early 1980s with hits such as "Sunday, Bloody Sunday," "Where the Streets Have No Name," and "I Still Haven't Found What I'm Looking For." U2 remained popular and influential through the 1980s, but by the early 1990s seemed passé. Then came a renaissance.

Starting around 1998, U2 became the number one band in Europe and the United States. Its members played both their old hits and a smattering of new ones, but more important, lead singer Bono became a spokesman for activism in the area of world poverty. Bono and his wife, Alison, had spent some time with dying Africans in the 1980s, and the event changed their lives. Bono thus became a tireless spokesman in the fight to eradicate radical poverty (by which he meant extreme poverty) during the past decade.

Many other rock stars have turned their attention to world issues, but Bono has become more influential than all of them combined. By the start of the new century, he was meeting regularly with heads of state, cajoling the United Nations, and traveling throughout the world to meet his goal of eradicating radical poverty.

Although other rock stars, such as Mick Jagger and Paul McCartney, had lasted longer on the public stage, Bono was by far the most influential of the bunch. He has become a genuine hero to Gen Xers and a source of admiration for baby boomers as well. He has, in fact, become the closest thing to an intergenerational hero that the Western world has seen in some time.

Born in 1924 and a decorated hero of World War II, Bush spoke the language of the generation that had provided nearly all of the presidents during the past 30 years. Although he was Yale-educated and very bright, Bush was sparing in his speech, sometimes to the point of being laconic. It was as though he wished his deeds would speak for him. On the other hand, Bill Clinton, who was born in 1946, spoke the language of the baby boomers: He was verbose, smart as a whip, and he cavorted with icons of pop culture such as Barbra Streisand and Larry King. In the spring of 1992, incumbent vice president Dan Quayle inaugurated a values debate that would help shape the election.

Speaking to the Commonwealth Club of San Francisco, Quayle lamented the lack of family values prevalent in American culture: "The poor you have always with you, Scripture tells us. . . . But in this dynamic, prosperous nation, poverty had traditionally been a stage through which people pass on their way to joining the great middle class. But the [current] underclass seems to be a new phenomenon."[32]

Vice President Quayle went on to deliver a number of statistics about the condition of black families in the United States, mentioning the high rate of illegitimate children and unemployed black men. Had he said only this, Quayle's speech would not have caused such a stir. The statistics were well known to almost everyone in the audience, but the real issue, everyone knew, was what could be done about them. Quayle went on, and toward the end of his speech he referenced a popular television program of the time called *Murphy Brown*. The lead role was played by actress Candace Bergen, whom Quayle lambasted: "It doesn't help matters when prime time TV has Murphy Brown—a character who supposedly epitomizes today's intelligent, highly paid, professional woman—mocking the importance of fathers,

During a May 1992 speech at the Commonwealth Club of San Francisco, Vice President Dan Quayle caused quite a stir. He stated that shows like *Murphy Brown* were contributing to the decay in moral values by showing that it was acceptable for women to raise children without a father.

by bearing a child alone, and calling it just another 'lifestyle choice.'"[33] What a storm was created by those 39 words!

Even though family values had been part of both the Democratic and Republican party platforms since about 1976, with very different emphasis by each party, the phrase itself had never caught on. Vice President Quayle changed that in this speech, and by the end of the year, American newspapers and magazines were practically littered with references to family values, family positions, antifamily values, and the like.

Suddenly everyone wanted to support family values. Some columnists lamented the rush toward government involvement in what they saw as an individual matter, but most notable people clamored to offer their own opinion on

RALPH REED: FORMER LEADER OF THE RELIGIOUS RIGHT

Compared to Jerry Falwell or Pat Robertson, Ralph Reed was the personification of youth. Reed was tapped as leader of the Christian Coalition of America for a number of reasons, including his fund-raising ability, but his earnest face and boyish looks definitely played a part in his dramatic rise to prominence.

Born in Virginia in 1961, Reed grew up very near the Christian Broadcast Network headquarters of Pat Robertson. His introduction to politics came in the 1976 presidential election between Jimmy Carter and Gerald Ford; by then, he was on his way to becoming an ardent young Republican. Studying at the University of Georgia, he thought he would become a historian, but after he graduated in 1984, he was quickly drawn into evangelical politics. Pat Robertson took note of the promising young man and chose him to be the leader of the Christian Coalition of America.

A natural politician, Reed saw that Moral Majority Inc. had failed because its leaders had drawn too much attention to the organization, thereby draining energy from what it was supposed to accomplish. From the beginning, Reed designed the Christian Coalition of America as a different kind of evangelical movement. Perhaps he studied the success of Martin Luther King and the Southern Christian Leadership Conference in the 1960s, or perhaps he intuitively sensed that a grassroots organization would do better than a top-heavy one. The Christian Coalition of America was a "bottom-up" organization with local chapters creating their own literature and designing their own campaigns. The point, of course, was to elect Christians to office.

Established in 1989, the coalition scored its greatest success in the off-year congressional elections of 1994. Although there were other issues on the table that year, including a plan for universal health care, Reed and the Christian Coalition of America clearly played a major role in ousting the Democrats from 40 years of majority rule in the House and Senate. If ever there was a moment when the Christian Right could claim that the Republican Party owed it favors, that time was in 1995.

Reed stepped down as head of the Christian Coalition in 1997. He moved to Georgia, where he lost a 2006 race for lieutenant governor.

the matter. By this time, Moral Majority Inc. had disbanded, but some of the issues it had raised during the 1980s were still prevalent. Moreover, there was a new organization that gained prominence, the Christian Coalition of America.

George Bush and Dan Quayle were both renominated at the 1992 Republican National Convention in Houston, Texas. Quayle's speech about *Murphy Brown* had changed the political atmosphere to the point where the idea of family values was an important theme at the convention. By contrast, Bill Clinton received the Democratic nomination at a convention that celebrated the arrival of the baby boomers as a major political force. The theme song of the Clinton campaign was "Don't stop thinking about tomorrow . . . it'll soon be here," by the rock group Fleetwood Mac. Clinton won by a plurality of 44 percent, but he had a comfortable margin in the Electoral College. For the first time in 12 years, the Democrats would control the White House.

8

The Clinton Years

Like Ronald Reagan and Dwight Eisenhower, Bill Clinton was an enormously influential president who seemed to have an impact on many aspects of American life. Like Reagan and Eisenhower, he served two consecutive terms, and by the time he had left office in 2001, he had practically become synonymous with the federal government. All things change, of course, and the Bill Clinton of today is much less visible than the Bill Clinton of 1993 to 2001. However, during those eight years he and his wife, Hillary, did much to symbolize the leadership of the nation and of the baby boom generation.

TWO FOR THE PRICE OF ONE

When inaugurated in 1993, Bill Clinton consciously built upon the legacy of John F. Kennedy: He wanted to have a deep impact on the psyche of Americans, as well as on the nation's policies. John Kennedy would forever be seen as the great leader in policy, while his wife, Jackie Bouvier Kennedy, was seen as the embodiment of personal style. One of the great differences between the Kennedy and Clinton presidencies, and between the America of 1961 and of 1993, was that the first lady's role had changed.

Born near Chicago, Illinois, in 1947, Hillary Rodham Clinton is a bright, forceful woman. She and Clinton had both graduated near the top of their class at Yale Law School. Unlike Jackie

When Bill Clinton defeated incumbent George H. W. Bush in the 1992 presidential election, many Democrats felt that they were getting two policy makers for the price of one. Clinton's wife, Hillary, served as president of the Wellesley College Government and went on to have a successful career as a lawyer after attending Yale Law School. Bill and Hillary are pictured here at the Old State House in Little Rock, Arkansas, shortly after Clinton was elected president in November 1992.

Kennedy, or almost any previous first lady, Mrs. Clinton was seen as a policy maker in her own right. As proof of this, President Clinton named her head of a task force to reform the nation's health insurance system, an effort that failed in late 1994. Many admirers of the Clintons believed that the election of 1992 had given the nation two brilliant leaders for the price of one.

Many critics of the Clintons believed that Mrs. Clinton should play a more traditional role in the White House, which meant staying out of policy making. Her leadership of the health care task force polarized the nation, helping to defeat the very proposals she and her husband supported. This was just the beginning.

The 1990 U.S. Census revealed, and the 2000 Census later confirmed, that American living arrangements were different from any previous period in the nation's history. In 1990, for example, the number of households with a single person, living alone, slightly exceeded the number of households with two parents and children. Such a statistic would have been unthinkable a few decades earlier. It is always difficult to sum up the qualities or characteristics of a people, but the following generalizations could be used to describe Americans in the 1990s: They were ambitious, hoping to move up the economic ladder; they were impatient with G.I. Generation leadership and eager to have a baby boomer in the White House; and they were cautiously optimistic about the nation's future, while being quite optimistic about their own future and that of their families.

Given such an array of characteristics, one might have thought that the Clinton presidency would have enjoyed unparalleled success. Instead, rather like the Eisenhower and Reagan administrations, the Clinton government achieved some surprising successes and also weathered some dismal defeats.

THE REPUBLICAN REVOLUTION

All through the early autumn of 1994, political analysts reported something strange or unusual on the horizon, but no one could quite express what it meant. After the congressional elections of November, many Democrats were swept out of office, and every single Republican incumbent won the bid for reelection. In a country that had been accustomed to Republican control of the White House from 1981 through 1993 and Democratic control of Congress from 1953 through 1994, everything was suddenly reversed.

A less savvy politician might have lost his way, but Bill Clinton proved relentlessly pragmatic and able to shift course. In January 1995, he declared in his State of the Union address that the era of Big Government was over, an open admission that the policies of 1960s liberalism had failed. Clinton pledged to work with the newly elected Republican Congress, especially on items of interest such as welfare reform and changes in the bankruptcy code. Before too long, many Republicans lamented that Bill Clinton had managed to take control of several of their signature issues. He was certainly a politician of rare ability.

The Republicans had their way for a year or two. Clinton signed into law the Welfare Reform Act of 1996 and moved to ease restrictions on banks and lending institutions. A significant percentage of the American population continued to dislike him. For them, Clinton and his wife represented the worst excesses of the baby boom generation. There was little that Clinton could do; he could not disavow his own age group. Therefore, he played to his natural constituency and easily won reelection in 1996, defeating Republican candidate Robert Dole, a member of the G.I. Generation.

There were some memorable campaign moments, such as during the Republican National Convention, where Robert Dole assailed Bill Clinton and other baby boomers as members of a generation that never sacrificed, never achieved, and never grew up. That Clinton won reelection with such ease indicated that Americans believed in his policies. Voters had given the nation a newly Republican Congress, and they had confirmed their choice of a baby boom Democrat as the nation's chief executive. This type of divided government might be bad for passing new policies, but it seemed very good from the point of view of business and the stock market.

UP, UP, AND AWAY

No previous part of U.S. economic history, not even the stock market boom of the mid-1920s, equaled the frenzy of financial speculation that emerged in the middle to late 1990s. Regular, workaday Americans looked at their stock portfolios with interest and amazement, while middle-class workers became upper class, at least on paper. The reasons were twofold: the Internet and the emerging world economy.

Established by the U.S. military during the cold war era of the late 1950s, the Internet became available for general use in the 1990s. Every American family that could afford a computer could use the World Wide Web to access information about things like stock prices, housing overseas, and education in their neighborhood. The home-based computer, linked to the World Wide Web, seemed to offer an almost limitless future of possibility.

Many young people quickly formed what were called dot-com companies, which were based on the speculative value of their shares. With a few notable exceptions, such as Federal Reserve Chairman, Alan Greenspan, Americans invested a good deal of money in the Internet and the new global economy. By 2000, about half of all American families were invested in the stock market; that figure had only been 25 percent a decade or two earlier. The results were stupefying: The Dow Jones Industrial Average went from about 4,000 in 1993 to nearly 13,000 in 2001, while the newly formed National Association of Securities Dealers Automated Quotations system (NASDAQ) for technology stocks zoomed to almost 5,000. In an era of such excitement, who had time to think about morals, values, or any of those tired old debates known as the culture wars? The answer was plenty of people.

SCANDAL AND IMPEACHMENT

In the winter of 1998, even as the dot-com economy was roaring along, it became public knowledge that President Clinton had probably had an affair with a 22-year-old White House intern named Monica Lewinsky from late 1995 to early 1996. The story became big news right away, partly because it tended to confirm many of the suspicions people had already entertained about Bill Clinton's morality, or lack thereof.

Clinton did not help his own case. Rather than admitting to the affair, he lied about it, both on television and under oath. His detractors had called him Slick Willie, but the nickname seemed more appropriate than ever as Americans watched their president perform all sorts of verbal gyrations in attempts to circumvent the truth. First he said he had not had "sexual relations" with Lewinsky, and then he attempted to redefine "sexual relations" so that oral sex would not be part of the equation. In one of the lowest of many embarrassing moments, the president responded to a question by replying that "it depends on what the meaning of the word 'is' is." Seldom had a president appeared so beleaguered.

In terms of family values, what matters most is how the American public responded to the growing scandal. From polls taken at the time, as well as from anecdotal evidence, it appears that Americans generally thought President Clinton to be a man of low character, but they also thought him to be a man of exceptional executive ability. As long as he kept the ship of state on the right course, they were inclined to ignore his personal misconduct.

In January 1998, Bill Clinton was accused of having an affair with White House intern Monica Lewinsky. Although Clinton initially denied the accusation, he did an about-face in August 1998, stating that he had an "improper physical relationship" with Lewinsky.

A BLAST OF OUTRAGE

In the same year that the scandal broke, the Free Press published William Bennett's *The Death of Outrage*. A former education policy maker during the Reagan years, Bill Bennett turned his pen on Bill Clinton in ways that would have made most people squirm:

THE FIRST FAMILY

The First Family, composed of President Clinton, his wife, Hillary Rodham Clinton, and their teenage daughter, Chelsea Clinton, was caught at the center of the storm around the Monica Lewinsky scandal.

The scandal was hard on all involved, but Mrs. Clinton probably suffered the most. Just two years earlier she had penned *It Takes a Village, and Other Lessons Children Teach Us*. Published by Simon & Schuster, the book had remade the first lady's image in several ways. Previously seen as a rather cold and perhaps heartless policy maker, she now came across as a loving, caring person who accentuated the human possibilities of every situation, instead of the technocratic ones. The American public was perhaps more divided about Mrs. Clinton's role than they were about Mr. Clinton's immorality. Should she "stand by her man" as a country and western song put it? Or should she ditch her philandering husband?

No one will ever know what intricate negotiations went on between the president and first lady, what promises were and were not made. But Mrs. Clinton made a clear choice to stand with her husband and preserve their marriage, a stance that earned her a good deal of sincere admiration, even from some people who did not like her otherwise.

Chelsea Clinton was protected as much as possible. A well-balanced young woman, she seemed as attached to both her parents as in the past, and she negotiated her way through the rest of her father's term in office quite well. People wondered how the strain created by the scandal might show up in her life at a later time, but they also had to ponder whether millions of other young Americans had had to deal with the same issue .

The First Family weathered the Monica Lewinsky scandal, but the office of the president would not be the same. Americans generally expressed less regard for elected officials in their position, and the quality of leadership seen throughout Washington, D.C.

It is time to acknowledge in public what we know to be true in private: adultery is a betrayal of a very high order, the betrayal of a person one has promised to honor.

It often shatters fragile, immensely important social networks (made up of spouses, children, extended family, and mutual friends). It violates a solemn vow. When it is discovered, acute emotional damage almost always follows, often including the damage of divorce.[34]

Bill Bennett was distressed that so many Americans seemed to be willing to let the president off the hook. He pointed out that this led to a type of moral relativism, under which anyone and everyone could be absolved of anything through what the German philosopher Dietrich Bonhoeffer had called the doctrine of cheap grace. Bennett did not make any comparisons to Christian Right leaders of the 1980s (see Chapter 6), but he did draw a parallel with former Colorado senator Gary Hart. When the news media revealed that Hart was having an affair, he withdrew from the presidential race and apologized profusely to his staff for letting them down. Bill Clinton had done nothing of the kind, said Bill Bennett.

IMPEACHMENT AND TRIAL

In December 1998, the House of Representatives impeached Bill Clinton for having lied under oath about his relationship with Monica Lewinsky. He thereby became only the second American president ever to be impeached. The discontent grew throughout the country, with many people pointing fingers at the Congressional Republicans, calling on them to come clean about their own personal lives. In fact, one of them resigned after it was discovered that he had had an affair.

The matter then went to the U.S. Senate. Chief Justice William Rehnquist presided over the 21-day Senate trial in early 1999. In the end, President Clinton was acquitted of all the charges on which he had been impeached; like President Andrew Johnson in 1868, President Clinton was impeached but not convicted.

SEINFELD AND FRIENDS

If *All in the Family* was the quintessential television program of the 1970s, then *Seinfeld* and *Friends* were the most-watched, and perhaps the most important, programs of the 1990s. If Archie Bunker and Michael Stivic were at each other's throats much of the time, then the sitcoms of the 1990s showed a very different kind of family, one composed of unrelated people choosing to live together.

Debuting in 1990, *Seinfeld* centered around a comedian playing himself and three of his close friends, who spent most of their time together. All four members of the quartet dated, but none of them did so seriously, and it seemed they would spend years, perhaps decades, in a sort of voyeuristic approach to life: watching, waiting, and hanging back from any sort of commitment.

Coming on air in 1994, *Friends* revolved around a group of six, all of them in their 20s, who dated, sometimes each other, but who found the reliability of close friends more important than the promise of commitment or married life. Less quirky and more mainstream than their *Seinfeld* counterparts, the actors and actresses of *Friends* seemed like they could be one's cousins, nephews, perhaps even oneself!

Seinfeld went off the air in 1998 and *Friends* in 2004, and millions of Americans looked for the next big hit or hits. One thing was for sure; Americans had not wearied of television. Although 50 years had passed since the appearance of *I Love Lucy* and *Leave It to Beaver*, television retained its unique hold on the American public.

The country remained in a state of semi-shock for a few weeks, but then things seemed to return to normal. Many people agreed that President Clinton was not the most moral man, but he was also the most successful chief executive since Ronald Reagan. Most wanted to let him serve out the remainder of his term in peace.

9

Crossing the Millennium

The new millennium began on January 1, 2000, or on January 1, 2001, as some chronological purists insisted. Americans from all walks of life saw the dawn of a new century as a major event, as did peoples throughout the world. As was true at the beginning of the twentieth century, many people expressed a good deal of optimism about America and the world at large, and they expected things to get better in all sorts of ways.

THE MILLENNIAL GENERATION

In 2000, authors Neil Howe and William Strauss published *Millennials Rising: The Next Generation*, their book about the generation of Americans born after 1982. Howe and Strauss had strong credentials to write such a book; they were the coauthors of *Generations: The History of America's Future, 1584 to 2069* (1991) and *13th Gen: Abort, Retry, Ignore, Fail?* (1993).

Howe and Strauss had developed and refined a generational approach to the study of history; they believed that American society and culture moved in a pattern that could be detected through generational study. Both men were baby boomers, but they had given a good deal of attention to the younger generation, the one known as Generation X, and now they turned their focus to the true youngsters of America: those born between 1982 and 2000. They found that millennials (1) adored their parents, who usually were baby boomers; (2) accepted the feminist revolution and the civil rights era as accomplished facts, and saw no need to continue those revolutions; (3) were very accepting of mixed-race marriages and increasingly accepting of the idea of gay and lesbian marriages; and (4) were personally optimistic, but feared many of the trends in America's economic future, especially the rising cost of housing.

One of the key components that distinguished millennials from Generation X children was that they were wanted as babies, as children, and as young adults. Birthrates rose around 1980 and stayed high into the early 1990s. It was a time in which signs like "Baby on Board" appeared on American automobiles, which were often family-sized vans and minivans. Something about American culture had turned decidedly more pro-child in the 1980s, the authors argued, and the millennial children were the beneficiaries of that change.

More than any previous generation of American youngsters, parents fussed over, worried about, and prodded millennials toward success. American society had become extremely competitive in the years since the first millennials were born, and their parents wanted to insure that their children had every advantage in the race for professional and economic success.

Howe and Strauss believed that the millennials were the next "Great Generation," one that would rise to a significant challenge as their grandparents, the G.I. Generation, had done during World War II. Not everyone shared this rosy view. Six years after the publication of *Millennials Rising*, Jean M. Twenge challenged Howe and Strauss in her book, *Generation ME*.

Twenge did not simply focus on the young people born after 1982 as Howe and Strauss had done, and she did not separate Generation X (1964–1982) from the Millennial

In contrast to their predecessors, Generation X, the millennial generation was welcomed with open arms by their parents. Initially appearing in 1984, Baby on Board signs were proudly displayed by parents in the windows of their cars, indicating that American society had once again become pro-child.

Generation (1982–2000). Combining the two groups in her book about the Me Generation, Twenge wrote about a very large number of adults and young adults who, in her view, had become increasingly self-absorbed:

> Strauss and Howe also argue that today's young people are optimistic. That is true of children and adolescents who have absorbed the cheerful aphorisms so common today. . . . Yet this optimism often fades—or even smashes to pieces—once Generation Me hits the reality of adulthood. If you are a Baby Boomer or older, you might remember the 1970 book *Future Shock*, which argued that the accelerating pace of cultural change left many people feeling overwhelmed. Today's young people, born after

this book was published, take these changes for granted and thus do not face this problem. Instead, we face a different kind of collision: Adulthood Shock. Our childhoods of constant praise, self-esteem boosting, and unrealistic expectations did not prepare us for an increasingly competitive workplace. . . . After a childhood of buoyancy, GenMe is working harder to get less.[35]

Born in 1971, Twenge was definitely part of the generation she described, and her revelations were often less than flattering. Young Americans, she declared, had been raised on a diet of high expectations; everyone expected to become a professional of some type and to earn a high income. This was validated by a major study in 1999 that revealed that most young Americans expected to earn more than $75,000 a year, at a time when the average salary of 30-year-olds was around $30,000. This generation did not match their high expectations with truly intensive preparation for the work-force; instead, they assumed that attending a brand-name college or university, perhaps an Ivy League one, would help them to simply rise to the professional class. There seemed to be no preparation or thought about less skilled and less academically motivated people at all.

Social trends, according to Twenge, revealed a curious mixture of hope and pessimism. Generation Me, she said, did not believe in working hard, because so many of its members found things to be out of their control. This was accelerated by the rising number of young people who were called "learning disabled." At the same time, Generation Me believed in equality on all levels, whether it meant of race, gender, politics, or lifestyle. This admirable focus on equality also meant very little discrimination in matters of style or taste, so virtually all sorts of behaviors were seen as normal or acceptable. In Chapter 6 of her book, entitled "Generation Prude Meets Generation Crude," Twenge contrasted the sexual mores of the baby boom generation with those of their children, Generation Me, and found that the difference could hardly have been more striking.

Hooking up, which referred to casual sex without any sort of commitment, had replaced dating as the most common form of interaction between young men and women, Twenge declared. Members of Generation Me tended to adore their parents, but sex was one area in which there was truly a new generation gap:

> Many Boomers are struck by how today's young people are so comfortable talking about sex. We know all the terms, and can say them with little embarrassment (except sometimes when talking to our parents) perhaps because

Members of the millennial generation, or Generation Me, believe in equality for all cultural groups, but are often self-absorbed and do not know the meaning of hard work. Here, a member of the millennial generation organizes CDs in a store in Denver, Colorado.

GenMe has grown up in a time of more relaxed gender roles, many of us have talked about sexual topics with friends of the other sex. Girls can ask boys what makes them get an erection, and boys can ask girls what turns them on.[36]

Whether it was sex, lifestyle choices, or the pursuit of a career and financial reward, Generation Me seemed to experience life in a radically different way from that of their parents. When asked about it, many Generation Me parents expressed concern about the freewheeling lives their children were leading.

HOUSING AND EDUCATION

If there were two concerns that sobered young people at the turn of the millennium, they were the high costs associated with housing and education. In no other economic area was the difference between young people of 2000 and those of 1965 or 1970 so dramatic.

In 1965 or 1970, when a smaller percentage of the population went to college, the average college student could reasonably expect to cover room, board, and tuition at a public college or university for $2,500 a year or less. In 2000 or 2005, the figure had risen to eight or even nine times that figure, and if one chose a private college or university, some cost as much as $40,000 a year. To be sure, loans were available to most, but these loans threatened to become millstones around the necks of young people. Who could truly afford to graduate from college owing $50,000 or more?

College debt was bad enough, but housing debt was simply ridiculous. The average price of an American home doubled and sometimes tripled between 1985 and 2005, while real wages remained nearly stagnant. Families needed places to live, but the market did not oblige. The double squeeze created by education and housing costs led a mother and daughter to coauthor *The Two-Income Trap: Why Middle-Class Mothers & Fathers are Going Broke.*

Elizabeth Warren and Amelia Warren Tyagi were prime examples of successful American women. The mother, Elizabeth, was a professor at Harvard Law School and the daughter, Amelia, had cofounded a health benefits firm. Mother and daughter wrote their book to highlight the economic distress that afflicted many American families. According to Warren and Tyagi, during the 1990s and early part of the new millennium there had been a fundamental shift in family economics as desperately stressed parents had to:

☆ Purchase incredibly high-priced homes in order for their children to attend good schools

☆ Go into debt so their children could attend good colleges and universities

☆ Risk bankruptcy time and again, just to give their children a decent chance in life

Warren and Tyagi declared that their research confirmed what many suspected, that the single greatest factor in a woman declaring bankruptcy tended to be whether or not she had children. In other words, what had once been the social safety net of father, mother, and children had become the economic danger zone of college debt, housing debt, and families at risk for bankruptcy. Warren and Tyagi wrote their book with a special mission to educate the public that middle-class families were going broke because of their real concern about their children's futures, not because of an imagined need to have many conveniences or status objects.

NEW DR. SPOCKS

Every generation since 1946 had witnessed the publication of books about babies, toddlers, and young adults, but the start of the new millennium exceeded all expectations. As children became more expensive and as homes and education became nearly impossible to finance, parents were still concerned with those early years of life: How best to raise Johnny, Suzy, or Joan?

There were literally hundreds of new books, with titles such as *Complete Baby and Child Care*, *The Baby Book: Everything You Need to Know About Your Baby from Birth to Age Two*, and so forth, but some of the most compelling came from the pen of Michael Gurian. A family therapist and founder of the Gurian Institute, he wrote *The Wonder of Boys*, *The Wonder of Girls*, *The Good Son*, and *Boys and Girls Learn Differently*. Perhaps his most defining work was published in 2007.

Nurture the Nature: Understanding and Supporting Your Child's Unique Core Personality was a book for the times. Gurian's thesis was that each child comes to the world with a slightly different set of dispositions, talents, and areas of difficulty, and that parents could not use a cookie-cutter approach to child rearing. Instead, parents needed to pay a great deal of attention to the core personality of each child, and thereby learn which behaviors and activities would be beneficial and which might be harmful. The title, *Nurture the Nature*, indicated Gurian's belief that each child was different by nature, and that parents could help or harm the progression of each child through specific activities, or nurture. Gurian employed a good deal of cognitive science, especially on brain development, to back up his thesis that chronic stress, both in families and in society as a whole, was harming the basic core personality of many children.

THE AMERICAN FAMILY IN 2007

In 2007, America was substantially different than it had been in 1946. The differences were both qualitative and quantitative. The 2000 Census showed that American families were

☆ Smaller in the past, sometimes with one or two children

☆ More diverse than in the past, with a steady growth in the number of mixed-race marriages

☆ Less easy to categorize than in the past, with a small but growing number of lesbian and gay families

The U.S. Census also revealed that the population as a whole was

☆ Much larger than in the past (it hit 300 million in 2006)

☆ Much more diverse than in the past, with whites accounting for only 65 percent of the total

☆ Less concentrated in the nuclear family than in the past

Family Values

Could anyone speak for family values in 2007?

Traditionalists, especially those who lived in red, or Republican states, spoke with nostalgia for the 1940s and 1950s. Traditionalists were on the defensive, however, as a number of their spokesmen and women came under fire for immoral behavior of their own.

Liberals and laissez-faire intellectuals also offered their opinions, especially those who spoke for blue, or Democratic states', values, but many who listened were skeptical. Had there not already been more than 30 years of liberal experiments?

Hard-edged social critics like Christopher Lasch were hard to find in 2007. They had been prominent in the 1960s and 1970s, but the increase of self-help books and the proliferation of media outlets made them less likely to be heard. If there was a Christopher Lasch in 2007, someone willing to take on all comers, it was Christopher Hitchens of *Vanity Fair*, and he wrote far more often on military, industrial, and political topics than on social ones.

CONCLUSION

America was still a family-based society in 2007, but many conservatives felt that the traditional mortality and values upheld by the family unit was no longer prevalent in American society. Single-parent families were commonplace, as was birth out of wedlock. The extended family, composed of grandparents, parents, and children, seemed a thing of the past, and even the nuclear family seemed in jeopardy. The family would have to survive in order for the population to continue, but what shape it would take was somewhat uncertain.

10

From Vertical to Horizontal

The American family of 1945, as painted by Norman Rockwell, had been a one-size-fits-all institution. Mother tended the home, father earned the money, and children grew to be adults in a world that was three-generational, in which many young people knew their grandparents. Even if one argues that the extended family was not as prevalent in 1945 as Rockwell seemed to suggest, we can still say with some confidence that the American family was vertically oriented: There was an order from top to bottom that proceeded from the wisdom of the elders, to the maturity of the middle-aged, to the energy and spiritedness of youth.

In his landmark book *The Sibling Society*, Robert Bly posited that the American family, indeed American society as a whole, had become horizontal. Everyone seemed on the same plane, with no more or less wisdom than anyone else. Middle-aged parents were people who just happened to be older than their children, and grandparents were often shunted off to nursing homes, where their wisdom was contained. The images of America described by Rockwell and Bly beg the question: Is there a central aspect to American families today?

The answer is no. Exposed to a bewildering array of lifestyle choices, and besieged by a media that finds interest only in the young and beautiful, the American family is no longer what it was in the days immediately after World War II. However, not all the losses need be lamented.

The American family of the early twenty-first century is much different than the traditional Norman Rockwell family of the first half of the twentieth century. Today, children are often disconnected with both their parents and their neighborhood.

The old system had a lot of oppressive aspects. Many people stayed in unhappy marriages from a lack of options, and some parents abused or neglected their children. Quite a few American families, whether composed of one parent or two, live happier, even healthier lives than their grandparents did in the 1940s. The most stunning change from the

Norman Rockwell days is not the change in family size and structure, but the loss of the neighborhood.

In Chapter 1, we heard about the Normal Rockwell painting that depicted neighborhood children playing in a tree and a pretty girl who seemed tailor-made for the returning soldier. Much of that was idealized, of course, but it suggested something quite real to Americans in the 1940s: The good things in life were close by, often found right where one lived. That cannot be said today.

Whether they are inner-city children facing poverty and the ugliness of tenements, or suburban children living in a sea of manicured lawns, the young people of today aspire to reach out to a wider world. This is done in all manner of ways, with the use of cell phones and the Internet heading the list. The good things in life exist, but today they may not be close at hand; instead, they may be found through travel, the computer, and long-distance conversations.

What this means is the decline of the neighborhood and the sense of belonging to a particular place. Families can, and do, survive without neighborhoods and the accompanying social interaction, but their lives are impoverished.

There is no way to turn the clock back to the 1940s, to return to a simpler and, apparently, easier time. Unless we make room for neighborhoods and for families to live in them, America will become the Sibling Society in all truth, a place where people belong to everyone and no one at the same time, a land where no one is responsible for anything, and yet everything cries out to be done.

CHRONOLOGY

1945   World War II ends; Norman Rockwell paints *The Homecoming*.

1946   Baby boom begins with 3.4 million babies born; *Common Sense Baby and Child Care* is published; *Understanding Marriage and the Family* is published.

1950   Television first appears in American homes.

1957   *Leave It to Beaver* debuts on television.

1960   The Pill is approved by the FDA; John F. Kennedy is elected after the first televised presidential debates.

Timeline

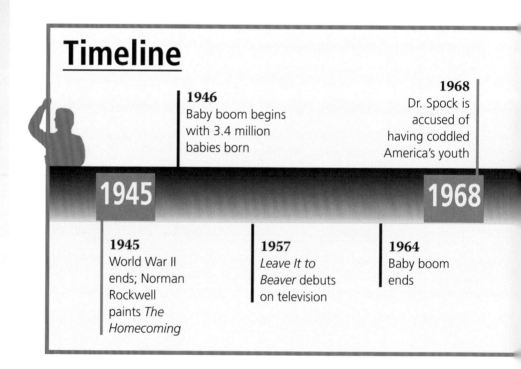

1946
Baby boom begins with 3.4 million babies born

1968
Dr. Spock is accused of having coddled America's youth

1945

1968

1945
World War II ends; Norman Rockwell paints *The Homecoming*

1957
Leave It to Beaver debuts on television

1964
Baby boom ends

1963	Betty Friedan's *The Feminine Mystique* is published; John F. Kennedy is assassinated in Dallas, Texas.
1964	American involvement in Vietnam escalates; baby boom ends; eldest of the baby boomers go off to college.
1967	Youth protests against the Vietnam War escalate.
1968	Dr. Spock is accused of having coddled America's youth.
1970	*Dare to Discipline*, by Dr. James Dobson, is published.
1971	*All in the Family* debuts on television.
1972	Congress approves the Equal Rights Amendment (ERA).
1973	Supreme Court rules in *Roe v. Wade*.

1970
Dare to Discipline,
by Dr. James Dobson,
is published

1973
Roe v. Wade

1976
Jimmy Carter
is elected
president; he is
the first born-
again Christian
to hold office

1970

1976

1971
*All in the
Family* debuts
on television

1972
Congress approves
the Equal Rights
Amendment (ERA)

1976	Jimmy Carter is elected president; he is the first born-again Christian to hold the highest office in the United States.
1979	Iran Hostage Crisis begins; Moral Majority Inc. is founded.
1980	White House Conference on Families takes place; Ronald Reagan is elected president.
1982	The Equal Rights Amendment fails to receive a two-thirds majority by the states.
1983	The word *yuppies* appears in the dictionary.
1987	Scandals break out in several ministries.
1988	George H. W. Bush wins the presidential election.
1990	*Time* notes the appearance of Generation X.
1992	Vice President Dan Quayle ignites discussion of family values; Bill Clinton wins the presidential election.

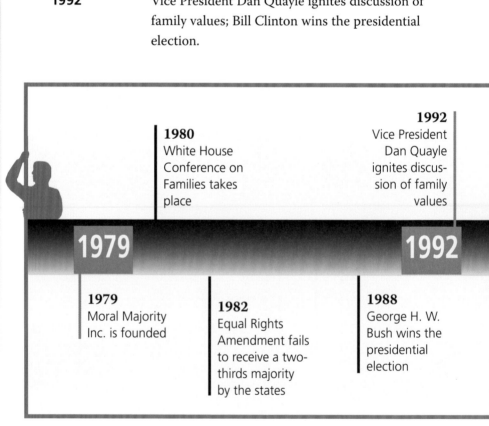

1993	Family and Medical Leave Act is approved and signed.
1994	Health Care Reform Task Force fails in its goal; Republicans win both houses of Congress in a landslide election.
1996	Bill Clinton wins reelection; Clinton signs Welfare Reform Act.
1998	Monica Lewinsky scandal breaks; House of Representatives impeaches Bill Clinton.
1999	President Clinton is acquitted by Senate.
2000	New millennium begins.
2006	U.S. population reaches 300 million.
2007	Michael Gurian's *Nurture the Nature* is published.

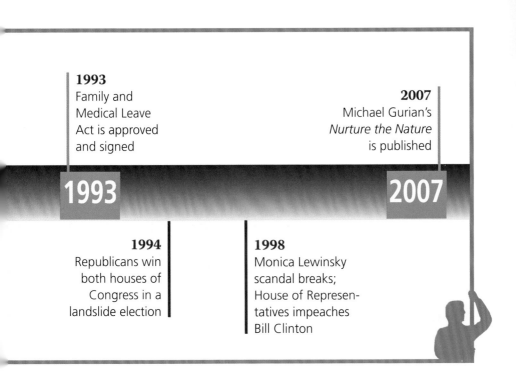

1993
Family and
Medical Leave
Act is approved
and signed

2007
Michael Gurian's
Nurture the Nature
is published

1993

2007

1994
Republicans win
both houses of
Congress in a
landslide election

1998
Monica Lewinsky
scandal breaks;
House of Represen-
tatives impeaches
Bill Clinton

NOTES

CHAPTER 1

1. Robert Bly, *The Sibling Society* (Boston: Addison-Wesley, 1996), 31.
2. Ibid., 32.
3. Ibid., 44–45.

CHAPTER 2

4. John B. Watson, *Psychological Care of Infant and Child* (New York: W.W. Norton, 1928), 81–82.
5. Carter, Susan B. et al. *Historical Statistics of the United States*, vol. 1 (Cambridge University Press, 2006), 392–93.
6. Benjamin Spock, *The Common Sense Book of Baby and Child Care* (New York: Duell, Sloan and Pearce, 1946), 3.
7. Watson, *Psychological Care of Infant and Child*, 12.
8. Ray V. Sowers and John W. Mullen, eds., *Understanding Marriage and the Family* (Chicago: Eugene Hugh, 1946), 11.
9. Ibid., 53.
10. Ibid., 63.

CHAPTER 3

11. Betty Friedan, *The Feminine Mystique* (New York: W.W. Norton, 2001), 15.
12. Ibid.
13. "Is Dr. Spock to Blame?" *Newsweek*, September 23, 1968, 68.
14. Ibid., 71.
15. Ibid., 71.

CHAPTER 4

16. James Dobson, *Dare to Discipline* (Carol Stream, Ill.: Tyndale House, 1970), 22.
17. Ibid., 22–23.
18. Ibid., 21.
19. Jimmy Carter, *Our Endangered Values: America's Moral Crisis* (New York: Simon & Schuster, 2005), 19.
20. White House Conference on Families, *Listening to America's Families: Action for the 80's* (Washington, D.C.: White House Conference on Families, 1980), 5.
21. Ibid., 159.

CHAPTER 5

22. Donald Bruce Johnson, *National Party Platforms of 1980* (Urbana, Ill.: University of Illinois Press, 1982), 182–183.
23. Ibid., 54.
24. Howell Raines, "Reagan Backs Evangelicals in Their

Political Activities," *New York Times*, August 23, 1980, 8.

25. Ibid.

26. Meg Greenfield, "The Feds and the Family," *Newsweek*, September 8, 1980, 88.

CHAPTER 6

27. Marjorie Garber, *Sex and Real Estate: Why We Love Houses* (New York: Pantheon Books, 2000), 17–18.

28. Hunter S. Thompson, *Generation of Swine: Tales of Shame and Degradation in the '80s* (New York: Simon & Schuster, 1988), 21.

CHAPTER 7

29. "Twentysomething," *Time*, July 16, 1990, 57.

30. Ibid.

31. Ibid.

32. Dan Quayle, *Standing Firm: A Vice-Presidential Memoir* (New York: HarperCollins, 1994), 382–383.

33. Ibid., 386.

CHAPTER 8

34. William J. Bennett, *The Death of Outrage: Bill Clinton and the Assault on American Ideals* (New York: Free Press, 1998), 21.

CHAPTER 9

35. Jean M. Twenge, *Generation ME: Why Today's Young Americans Are More Confident, Assertive, Entitled—and More Miserable Than Ever Before* (New York: Free Press, 2006), 7.

36. Ibid., 165.

BIBLIOGRAPHY

Bennett, William J. *The Death of Outrage: Bill Clinton and the Assault on American Ideals*. New York: Free Press, 1998.

Bly, Robert. *The Sibling Society*. Boston: Addison-Wesley, 1996.

Clinton, Hillary Rodham. *It Takes a Village, and Other Lessons Children Teach Us*. New York: Simon & Schuster, 1996.

Davis, Patti. *The Way I See It*. New York: G.P. Putnam's Sons, 1992.

Dobson, James. *Dare to Discipline*. Carol Stream, Ill.: Tyndale House, 1970.

Garber, Marjorie. *Sex and Real Estate: Why We Love Houses*. New York: Pantheon Books, 2000.

Gurian, Michael. *Nurture the Nature: Understanding and Supporting Your Child's Unique Core Personality*. Hoboken, N.J.: Jossey-Bass Books, 2007.

Howe, Neil, and William Strauss. *Millennials Rising: The Next Great Generation*. New York: Vintage Books, 2000.

———. *13th Gen: Abort, Retry, Ignore, Fail?* New York: Vintage Books, 1993.

Hymowitz, Kay S. *Marriage and Caste in America: Separate and Unequal Families in a Post-Marital Age*. Chicago: Ivan R. Dee, 2006.

Lasch, Christopher. *Haven in a Heartless World: The Family Besieged*. New York: Basic Books, 1997.

Smith, Norris, ed. *Changing U.S. Demographics*. New York: H.W. Wilson, 2002.

Sowers, Ray V., and John W. Mullen, eds. *Understanding Marriage and the Family*. Chicago: Eugene Hugh, 1946.

Spock, Benjamin. *The Common Sense Book of Baby and Child Care*. New York: Duell, Sloan and Pearce, 1946.

Taffel, Ron, and Melinda Blau. *The Second Family: How Adolescent Power Is Challenging the American Family*. New York: St. Martins Press, 2001.

Thompson, Hunter S. *Generation of Swine: Tales of Shame and Degradation in the '80s.* New York: Simon & Schuster, 1988.

Twenge, Jean M. *Generation ME: Why Today's Young Americans Are More Confident, Assertive, Entitled—and More Miserable Than Ever Before.* New York: Free Press, 2006.

Warren, Elizabeth, and Amelia Warren Tyagi. *The Two-Income Trap: Why Middle-Class Mothers & Fathers Are Going Broke.* New York: Basic Books, 2003.

Watson, John B. *Psychological Care of Infant and Child.* New York: W. W. Norton, 1928.

FURTHER READING

Bly, Robert. *The Sibling Society*. Boston: Addison-Wesley, 1996.

Clinton, Hillary Rodham. *It Takes a Village, and Other Lessons Children Teach Us*. New York: Simon & Schuster, 1996.

Howe, Neil, and William Strauss. *Millennials Rising: The Next Great Generation*. New York: Vintage Books, 2000.

Spock, Benjamin. *The Common Sense Book of Baby and Child Care*. New York: Duell, Sloan and Pearce, 1946.

Time-Life Books. *The Digital Decade: The 90s*. Time Life, 2000.

Time-Life Books. *Pride and Prosperity: The 80s*. Time Life, 1999.

Twenge, Jean M. *Generation ME: Why Today's Young Americans Are More Confident, Assertive, Entitled—and More Miserable Than Ever Before*. New York: Free Press, 2006.

WEB SITES

The Christian Coalition of America
http://cc.org/

Dan Quayle's Speech on Family Values
http://www.mfc.org/pfn/95-12/quayle.html

Family Values as Political Concept
http://www.mothersmovement.org/features/family_values/family_values.htm

PICTURE CREDITS

INDEX

ABOUT THE CONTRIBUTORS

Born in 1961, author **SAMUEL WILLARD CROMPTON** is right on the cusp between the baby boomers and Generation X. He lives and works in the Berkshire Hills of his native western Massachusetts, and he is the author or editor of many books, including a number written for Chelsea House. Crompton also is a major contributor to the *American National Biography* (1999).

Series editor **TIM McNEESE** is associate professor of history at York College in York, Nebraska, where he is in his sixteenth year of college instruction. Professor McNeese earned an associate of arts degree from York College, a bachelor of arts in history and political science from Harding University, and a master of arts in history from Missouri State University. A prolific author of books for elementary, middle and high school, and college readers, McNeese has published more than 90 books and educational materials over the past 20 years, on everything from Picasso to landmark Supreme Court decisions. His writing has earned him a citation in the library reference work *Contemporary Authors*. In 2006, he appeared on the History Channel program *Risk Takers/History Makers: John Wesley Powell and the Grand Canyon.*